Wild Truth Bible Lessons

pictures of God 2

12 more wild Bible studies
on the character of a wild God—
and what it means for your
junior highers & middle schoolers

Check out these great *Wild Truth* books for your junior highers and middle schoolers!

Wild Truth Journal for Junior Highers
with companion curriculum
Wild Truth Bible Lessons
Wild Truth Bible Lessons 2

Wild Truth Journal—Pictures of God
with companion curriculum
Wild Truth Bible Lessons—Pictures of God
Wild Truth Bible Lessons—Pictures of God 2

pictures of God 2

Wild Truth Bible Lessons

12 more wild Bible studies
on the character of a wild God—
and what it means for your
junior highers & middle schoolers

Mark Oestreicher

TO 20
P·R·E·S·S

ys
Youth Specialties

ZondervanPublishingHouse
Grand Rapids, Michigan

A Division of HarperCollinsPublishers

Wild Truth Bible Lessons—Pictures of God 2: 12 more wild Bible studies on the character of a wild God—and what it means for your junior highers and middle schoolers

Copyright © 2001 by Youth Specialties

Youth Specialties Books, 300 S. Pierce St., El Cajon, CA 92020, are published by Zondervan Publishing House, 5300 Patterson Ave. S.E., Grand Rapids, MI 49530.

Library of Congress Cataloging-In-Publication Data

Oestreicher, Mark.
    Wild truth Bible lessons—pictures of God 2 : 12 more wild Bible studies on the character of a wild God—and what it means for your junior highers and middle schoolers / Mark Oestreicher.
        p. cm.
    ISBN 0-310-22366-0
    1. God—Biblical teaching. 2. Christian education of teenagers. I. Title.

    BS544 .O47 2001
    268'.433—dc21

                                                                    00-043878

Unless otherwise indicated, all Scripture quotations are taken from the *Holy Bible: New International Version* (North America Edition). Copyright © 1973, 1978, 1984 by International Bible Society. Used by permission of Zondervan Publishing House.

Edited by Lorna McFarland Hartman
Illustrations by Krieg Barrie
Design by Patton Brothers Design
Interior layout by Tom Gulotta

Printed in the United States of America

01 02 03 04 05 06 / VG / 10 9 8 7 6 5 4 3 2 1

For my sisters, Lori and Lisa. What a blessing you are. I'm proud to be your little brother.

Contents

Delight yourself in the Lord and he will give you the desires of your heart. **Dream big about how God can use you.**

I am the Light of the world. Whoever follows me will never walk in darkness, but will have the light of life. **You can bring light into the darkness.**

I am the resurrection and the life. He who believes in me will live, even though he dies. **God gives life, and you can share it with others.**

He will be like rain falling on a mown lawn, like showers watering the earth. **God can use you like rain—to nourish, clean, refresh, and cool others.**

Look, the Lamb of God, who takes away the sin of the world! **Be like Jesus by giving a part of yourself—your time, talents, gifts, money—for others.**

How great is the love the Father has lavished on us, that we should be called children of God! **You receive unconditional love from the Father; now pass it along!**

I am the bread of life. **You can help others satisfy their hunger for God.**

But you are a chosen people, a royal priesthood, a holy nation, a people belonging to God. **God has included you on his team, and he wants you to include others, too.**

Greater love has no one than this, that he lay down his life for his friends. **You can share with others what God has shared with you.**

I will lead the blind by ways they have not known, along unfamiliar paths I will guide them. **You can trust God to lead you the right way.**

I am the Lord, your Holy One, Israel's Creator, your King. **God has all the good qualities of a king, and you can, too.**

The Word became flesh and made his dwelling among us. **When God became human, he made a difference in the world. Now you can make a difference in the world.**

Acknowledgments

As always, I thank my amazing wife, Jeannie, and the world's best kids, Liesl and Max, for all your support and encouragement.

Thanks to the killer product department at YS—great coworkers and great friends.

Thanks to my friend Laura Gross for all her help with this project.

And thanks to the fine people at the Bethel West Seminary library where I spent my writing days. Your ignoring my illegal thermos of coffee made this project possible.

What God Looks Like

Ever stop to wonder why there are no original portraits of God in the Bible? When the Almighty made those spectacular Old Testament appearances, didn't anyone stop and say, "This would look great as a painting"? Maybe they were too busy holding on for dear life. But surely someone among Jesus' followers knew how to sketch a likeness of him. Unfortunately, we have no drawings to prove it.

Raised on faded filmstrips and flickering TV images, I'm accustomed to *seeing* really important stuff, like the anatomy of a molecule and whether Gilligan will ever get off the island. It seems to me that details about God—who he is, what he looks like, what he did—rank highest among what most deserves a picture.

God agrees. But instead of using sketches and paintings, he chose another powerful medium to convey his image: *words*. The Bible is a *word-picture* book of God. Each word-picture reveals something important about God's character so we might get to know him better. And catch a glimpse of what *we'll* look like someday...if we let him do his work on us.

This book is a guide to a dozen pictures of God. It's designed to help you reveal these pictures to your junior high students so they can get to know God better and become more like him. Here's how the lessons are organized:

Grabs your students' attention to prepare them for what's ahead.

Takes your group into the Bible to catch God in the act of revealing his character.

Explores what this character would look like in young teen skin.

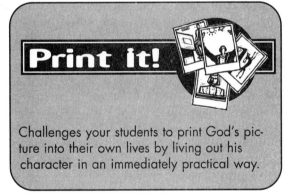

Challenges your students to print God's picture into their own lives by living out his character in an immediately practical way.

Within each of the above lesson segments, you'll find games, activities, dramatic pieces, handouts, and options. Don't try to use everything: You know your students best, so use just what you know will work for *them*, and adapt or discard the rest.

This is the sixth book in the Wild Truth line, so if you like this one, be sure to check out the others. All are designed to help you develop godly character in the lives of junior high students. If you're looking for a great way to expand your lessons beyond the classroom, check out *Wild Truth Journal: Pictures of God*. This junior high devotional contains short lessons based on 50 God-pictures, including the dozen covered here. On their own, students can continue their discovery and emulation of God's character, even after you've run out of lessons from this book. And for 12 more God-picture lessons, pick up a copy of *Wild Truth Bible Lessons: Pictures of God*.

All the books in the Wild Truth line are written by my friend Mark Oestreicher, the oldest junior higher I know. Mark's refreshing perspective and quirky sense of humor betray his long and passionate commitment to reaching this age group with the wild truth about God.

May you revel in this Wild Truth yourself while sharing it with your students.

Todd Temple
10 TO 20 Press

God is like a DREAMER

Delight yourself in the Lord and he will give you the desires of your heart. Commit your way to the Lord; trust in him and he will do this. —*Psalm 37:4-5*

Goals

STUDENTS WILL—

- Learn the difference between helpful and hurtful dreaming.
- Understand that God is a dreamer, dreamed up dreaming, and wants to give us our dreams.
- Dream about how God might use them.

Picture Prep

Dream of a land...

Have students get into groups of three or four. Ask them to imagine an island where there are no influences from the outside world, unless they want them. As a group, they have to dream up the whole culture, including the following items (write these on a whiteboard, if possible)—

- A name for this new country
- A motto for the country's flag
- The national sport
- Five laws
- Five subjects taught in school

After all the groups are done, have them present their new countries and cultures to the whole group. Make sure you don't let kids tease or ridicule the work of another group—some will be nervous about sharing their answers.

Then ask—

You'll Need—

- Blank paper
- Pencils or pens
- Whiteboard and markers (optional)

What's a dream?
Most young teens will initially think of the kind of dreams people have when sleeping. But they should also realize that a dream is something you hope for or long for.

Why do people dream, not the night-time kind of dream, but the hope-for kind?
Because they want something better or different. They want their lives to change.

Is this kind of dreaming good or bad?
Your kids will probably expect there to be a right answer on this question, and might be cautious in answering. Really, dreaming can be good or bad, depending on the focus of the dream.

If someone dreams of having sex all the time, well, I think we can agree that's not good dreaming—it's called lust! If someone dreams of blowing up the capitol building, I think we can safely say that's not good dreaming either.

But a dream about who you might become or what you might do in life—that's probably good. A dream about how God might use you? Definitely good!

Whenever a whiteboard is used, you can substitute a chalkboard (don't forget the chalk), flip chart, butcher paper taped to the wall, or, in some cases, a PowerPoint setup.

Action shot

God the dreamer

Pass out copies of **God the Dreamer** (page 15) and pens or pencils (or markers or crayons or eyeliner pencils or caulking guns) to each student. If you're using both **God the Dreamer** and **Dream On!** (page 16) in the next activity, it would be great if you could copy them back-to-back.

You make the call: if your kids are restless, you might want to just work through this sheet orally. And if your students just hate handouts and regularly shred them or turn them into an entire paper air force, all the questions on this sheet could be done orally or discussed in small groups. But if you think they can focus, have them work in pairs or trios to fill in answers on this sheet.

If you work through the questions out loud, you'll obviously debrief it as you go. But if you have the kids work on their own, make sure you pull them back together and debrief their answers. Ask for a few responses to the questions on the sheet. And ask—

You'll Need—

- A copy of **God the Dreamer** (page 15)
- Pencils or pens

☼ What are some other cool things God dreamed up?
Get lots of answers.

☼ What if God wasn't a dreamer? How might our world be different?
Just let your students get creative here. Hopefully, they'll come up with things like these: There might only be one kind of animal—we'd just call it animal...We might not be female and male—just people, with some boring way of reproducing...The earth might be brown and flat all over...

☼ What dreams do you think God still has for the world?
Don't just settle for quick churchy answers here—that people would know him. Yes, that's true; but push kids farther. What are some of God's dreams that are not fulfilled? Justice for the poor...A witness for him in every people group...That we would love and respect the earth he made for us...

Self-portrait

Dream teens

Help kids think about the difference between helpful and hurtful dreaming. This is a bit different than just asking if a dream is *good* or *bad*. Life isn't always that clear-cut. But we can help kids think critically about whether their dreams are encouraging, bring them hope, and line up with God's desires, or whether they're selfish and destructive. Explain that the Bible cautions us to be careful what we spend our time thinking about. So there's some dreaming that God loves, and some that's hurtful to us, and not honoring to God

Read the five case studies in this section. After each one, discuss with your students whether the main character's dreaming was helpful or hurtful.

I'm Martin, and I have this dream of becoming an artist. I know it's a long shot, and that not too many people can actually earn a living as a painter or an illustrator. And I might not get to do it. Or I might be a graphic designer or something like that, which would still be cool. I'd really love to spend my life drawing and painting.

☼ Is Martin's dream helpful or hurtful?
It's great. Whether he knows it or not, Martin's desire is to use the abilities God has given him.

My name's Bethany, and I have this dream. It's a little embarrassing, and I don't tell very many people. I'd like to be a really popular movie star. I'd love to have people know who I am, and have my picture show up all over the place.

Is Bethany's dream helpful or hurtful?

It's hurtful. Her dream is basically a selfish cry for attention. You might want to ask this follow-up question:

How can two people both dream of going into an acting career, and one dream be helpful and the other one hurtful?

The answer revolves around motive. To dream of acting because you love acting is a great thing. But to dream of acting so you'll be popular or rich is a destructive dream.

My name is Shenika, and I dream about having grandparents. All my grandparents died before I was born. And most of my friends have really cool grandparents. I feel like I got ripped off.

Is Shenika's dream helpful or hurtful?

If she spends her time moping and feeling sorry for herself, it could be hurtful. But if she's just dreaming out of the longing of her heart, this can be a great dream. Maybe God will provide someone who can be like a grandparent for her.

I'm Alfonso, I dream all the time about having tons of money. My family doesn't have much money, and so that makes it even worse. I dream of the cars I'd buy, the house I'd live in, the clothes I'd wear, and other stuff I'd own. Wow! That would just be so great.

Is Alfonso's dream helpful or hurtful?

Hurtful. Dreaming of having enough to not be poor is

one thing, but focusing on money to have more and more material things can be very hurtful to the dreamer.

Hello, my name is Bassam. My family moved to the United States a couple years ago. It's been pretty tough for me. I'm doing fine in school and everything, but I can't seem to make any friends. So, I guess that's my dream: to have one or two friends.

Is Bassam's dream helpful or hurtful?

This is a good dream—God wants us to have friends.

Hopefully, after you've discussed these five case studies, your students will have a loose mental grasp of the difference between the kind of dreaming that God loves and the kind of dreaming that God doesn't like because it's hurtful to the dreamer. And if your students have *more* than a loose mental grasp of this idea, then, with awe and reverence, we give you the Young Teen Teacher of the Year Award! (Or you're just delusional!)

Print it!

Dream on!

Pass out copies of **Dream On!** (page 16). Your students should already have pens or pencils, if you used them for the last exercise. Of course, if they're anything like the junior highers I work with, half of those pencils now have broken tips, and half of the pens have been dismantled (and two boys have large quantities of blue ink on their hands). Oh well.

Ask your students to work on their own for a few

You'll Need—

A copy of **Dream On!** (page 16)

Pencils or pens

minutes. Circulate around the room to make sure your students understand what they're supposed to be doing. No matter how many times you clarify this, you'll probably still have a couple concrete thinkers who write down a nightmare they had last night as one of their dreams.

If your group has more than 10 students, ideally you'd be able to divide them into groups of about five—each with an adult leader—to have kids share their answers. This would offer a slightly safer atmosphere when they share these rather personal dreams. If you have to debrief in a large group format, make sure you're very careful to affirm answers and don't allow any teasing or snickering. Having your dreams mocked can do life-long damage—seriously!

Make sure you close your time in prayer, thanking God for honoring our dreams, and asking him for guidance to line up our dreams with his thinking.

Room decoration option

It's a great idea to create a large graphic symbol from each lesson for the wall of your room. The symbols represent the pictures of God that the group looks at each week. When you leave them as a collage on the wall over a period of weeks, they serve as a memory device and reminder of where you've been.

For this lesson, consider making a large graphic of a cartoon thought-bubble. It looks like a cloud—a scallop-edged oval—with two or three small ovals below it leading to the character who's speaking. They're used in cartoons to represent someone's thoughts.

God the Dreamer

Which of these things did God dream up?

- ❏ snails
- ❏ string cheese
- ❏ adverbs
- ❏ large intestines
- ❏ stuffed-crust pizza
- ❏ hummingbirds
- ❏ itty-bitty babies
- ❏ baseball
- ❏ running
- ❏ thumbtacks

- ❏ long-stemmed roses
- ❏ peach pits
- ❏ armpits
- ❏ trash pits
- ❏ kitty litter
- ❏ swamps
- ❏ fire
- ❏ barf
- ❏ night-time dreaming
- ❏ daydreaming

- ❏ puddles
- ❏ snow blowers
- ❏ summertime
- ❏ oil spills
- ❏ language
- ❏ families
- ❏ dust bunnies
- ❏ meatless hamburgers
- ❏ you
- ❏ a way to save you from hell!

Read Genesis 1. Make a list of the things God dreamed of, then made.

What difference does it make that God loves to dream—that he's a really good dreamer who dreams of amazing, outrageous things?

Dream On!

Psalm 37:4-5 says, "Delight yourself in the Lord and he will give you the desires of your heart. Commit your way to the Lord; trust in him and he will do this."
   Rewrite that in your own words.

God wants you to be a dreamer! It's a reflection of him that you *can* dream. What are three to five dreams that you have? (Remember, we're not talking about sleeping dreams—we're talking about the hopes of your heart!)

1.

2.

3.

4.

5.

What's the most radical thing you can imagine God using you to do anytime during your life?

What's the most radical thing you can imagine God doing through you this year?

What's a radical thing you can imagine God doing through you this week?

God is like a LiGHT

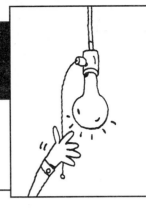

I am the Light of the world. Whoever follows me will never walk in darkness, but will have the light of life.
—John 8:12

Goals

STUDENTS WiLL—

- Think about the different things light does.
- See the *light* in God's character and in their own.
- Choose a specific *light-like* action to accomplish this week.

Picture Prep

whole meeting time on this exercise! Make sure you affirm all the teams and that the teams watch and pay attention to all the other performances.

Light dramas

Divide your group into teams of three to 10. (Yeah, I know that's a huge range, but I'm counting on you to know if your group is small or large). You'll want to get as close as you can to five teams. But don't freak if you only have three! Just adapt.

Give each team one assignment slip from **Light Dramas** (page 20). Instruct the groups that they'll have about five minutes to put together a short drama around the theme on their slip.

Walk around the room to make sure the teams understand what they're supposed to be doing. After about five minutes, or when it seems most of the teams are ready, have them perform their dramas for the whole group.

If you have a lot of teams, you'll need to keep the activity moving or you'll spend your

You'll Need—

- A copy of **Light Dramas** (page 20), cut into strips

Active option
Sardines

If your meeting time is in the evening, after dark, and if you have access to lots of rooms, hallways, stairwells, and the like, this classic youth group game is a great way to set up a discussion on the subject of light.

Choose one person to be It. That person has a couple minutes to go hide somewhere. Turn out all the lights—this game is only fun if you're able to make your playing area dark. Now, in a reverse of hide-and-seek, the rest of the students should try to find the person who's hiding. As they do, they should join the hiding person, keeping as quiet as possible. The last person to find the hiders is It for the next round.

Afterward, talk about the effect darkness—or the lack of light—had on the game. Talk about the different things light does.

You'll Need—

- Darkness—it needs to be nighttime
- The run of your facility

Action shot

Self-portrait

God-light

Hand out copies of **God-Light** (page 21) and pens or pencils to each student. (If your students are completely averse to handouts, this exercise could be done in small groups—with a leader in each group—or in a large group with you facilitating.) Make sure they have Bibles also (if they didn't bring them, you'll need to provide at least one for every other student).

Explain that the Scriptures listed on the handout are just a few of the verses where God describes himself as Light. Working in pairs, students write a sentence or two after each verse describing what the image of God as light in that verse tells us.

After a few minutes, have students share some of their answers. Then ask these questions—

You'll Need—

ö A copy of **God-Light** (page 21)

ö Bibles

ö Pencils or pens

ö **Now that you've seen examples in the Bible of God calling himself light, how would you say God is like light?**

ö **What difference does it make to us that God is like light?**

Light people

Make a transition from the concept of light to the idea that people can be like light. Start by asking this difficult question—

ö **How can people be like light?**

Realize that some of your students will still be functioning with very concrete thinking ability, and this abstract question might be a bit beyond their grasp! That's okay; you're just introducing the concept.

You'll Need—

ö Four volunteer readers

ö A copy of **Light People** (page 22) for each reader

Now ask for four volunteers to read case studies (two guys and two girls). Give each of these volunteers a story from the **Light People** (page 22). Ask them to read their stories for the whole group.

Then ask your group to order the four characters from the *most* like light to the *least* like light.

Here's a little insider information: there's no correct order of which character is *lighter* than another. They're all examples of being like light. But don't tell your kids. Let them state opinions and dialogue about them—it will help them process the very abstract idea of being like light.

Print it!

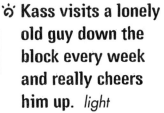

Light I am

Remind your students that since we're children of God, created in his image, God's character can be developed in us. That means we should be able to be light also. Have your students turn in their Bibles to Matthew 5:14-16 and see what Jesus has to say about his children being light.

Ask your students for ideas about how young teens can be like lights. Don't let them off easy on this—expect them to come up with answers. Ask follow-up questions to simplistic answers to try to ferret out deeper, more thoughtful answers.

Now check for understanding by reading this list of statements. Tell students that as soon as you finish each sentence, they should yell out *Light* or *Not light*, to describe whether or not the student in the sentence is reflecting this picture of God. They shouldn't wait to hear how other people are responding—they should just yell out an answer as soon as they have an idea.

You'll Need—

- Blank paper or index cards
- Pencils or pens
- Bibles

- **Shana decided she should tell the truth about something she'd been covering up.** *light*
- **Seth turned on the light in his room.** *not light*
- **Ginny helped her friend understand what it means to be a Christian.** *light*

- **Kass visits a lonely old guy down the block every week and really cheers him up.** *light*
- **Tori can't keep a secret and says, "That stuff just shouldn't stay hidden."** *not light*
- **Ben knows what the best decision is for everyone and he tells them his opinions.** *not light*
- **Alma helped her friend make a tough decision by talking with her about all the possible consequences of each choice.** *light*
- **Andrew likes to say encouraging things to people.** *light*

> You are the light of the world. A city on a hill cannot be hidden. Neither do people light a lamp and put it under a bowl. Instead they put it on its stand, and it gives light to everyone in the house. In the same way, let your light shine before men, that they may see your good deeds and praise your Father in heaven.
> —Matthew 5:14-16

Wrap up your time by handing out blank half-sheets of paper or index cards. Ask students to think of a specific situation where they could be like light in the next couple days. Tell them it can't be something general like, "I'll encourage people," or "I'll tell the truth." It has to name a person, a time, and a place.

After students write out their ideas, have several of them share with the group. Use this time to help them refine their plans of action—if they're too broad, ask them clarifying questions to get the plan down to a specific action.

Make sure you close in prayer, thanking God for being light to us and asking him for courage and wisdom to be light to the world.

Room decoration option

If you're using the room decoration idea described at the end of the first session, add a large graphic of a light bulb to the wall in your meeting space.

Light Dramas

Create a short (1-2 minutes) drama on how light reveals *truth*—showing how things really are.

- -

Create a short (1-2 minutes) drama on how light provides *warmth*.

- -

Create a short (1-2 minutes) drama on how light helps you see things *clearly*.

- -

Create a short (1-2 minutes) drama on how light can *give direction* and help you see which way you should go.

- -

Create a short (1-2 minutes) drama on how light gets rid of *darkness*.

God-Light

The Bible uses the word *light* over 200 times! And a whole bunch of those describe God as light. Here are a handful of those verses. After each one, write a sentence or two that describes what the verse has to say about this picture of God.

He is like the light of morning at sunrise on a cloudless morning, like the brightness after rain that brings the grass from the earth. (2 Samuel 23:4)

How is God like light in this verse?

By day the Lord went ahead of them in a pillar of cloud to guide them on their way and by night in a pillar of fire to give them light, so that they could travel by day or night. Neither the pillar of cloud by day nor the pillar of fire by night left its place in front of the people. (Exodus 13:21-22)

How is God like light in this verse?

You are my lamp, O Lord; the Lord turns my darkness into light. (2 Samuel 22:29)

How is God like light in this verse?

Send forth your light and your truth, let them guide me. (Psalm 43:3)

How is God like light in this verse?

When Jesus spoke again to the people, he said, "I am the light of the world. Whoever follows me will never walk in darkness, but will have the light of life." (John 8:12)

How is God like light in this verse?

(21)

Light People

My name is Stacey. Let me tell you what happened the other day. I was talking with my friend, Laura, and she was telling me about this guy at school and some stuff he'd done. And I knew the story wasn't true. So I said, "Hey Laura, what you're saying about him just isn't true." I guess I was sorta shining light on the truth.

- -

I'm Cody, and I guess I was like light the other day. My mom was trying to decide whether she should go on a date with this guy or not. I helped her look at both choices and make a good decision—she decided to go on the date. By helping her see the right way to go, I was a light for her.

- -

Hi, I'm Cassandra. I came home from school the other day and did something pretty radical—I cleaned my room! I don't just mean that I straightened it up. I mean I *cleaned* it. I threw out stuff that might not please God—some magazines with trashy articles, a note from a friend that was full of gossip, and even a CD. I got all that darkness out of my room!

- -

Hey, I'm Phil. My youth leader told me I was like light last weekend on our retreat. I don't really know what she meant—but I'll tell you what happened. All six guys on the retreat were having a big fight. It wasn't a physical fight—they were just being really mean to each other and ignoring each other. It was going to ruin the weekend. So I got everyone together, told them they better cut it out or they were going to have a lousy weekend. Then I made a joke and they all laughed. That seemed to break the ice. My youth leader said I brought warmth to a cold situation, like light. Whatever.

God is like LiFE

I am the resurrection and the life. He who believes in me will live, even though he dies. —*John 11:25*

Goals

STUDENTS WiLL—

- Understand the abstract idea of being life-giving.
- Catch God (as Jesus) in the act of being life-giving.
- Make a gutsy plan of action to be life-giving to someone this week.

Picture Prep

Life commercials

Divide your group up into teams of, well, some size! If your group is a dozen kids or less, you'll want to use teams of four-ish. If your group is bigger, you could make the teams as large as a dozen each.

Tell each team they'll have five minutes to put together a 30-second TV commercial for the concept of *life*. Not Life cereal! *Life* as opposed to *death*. Some of them will undoubtedly have a wonderfully confused and blank look on their faces at this point—cool, huh? That's good—they'll struggle with this abstract concept. But it will force them to think about what life is and what it represents. And that's a good start!

The teams will probably need more than five minutes to put together their commercials. Give

You'll Need—

☞ A couple of neutral judges and a food prize for the winning team—may I suggest squid? (optional)

them about seven or eight, or until it seems most of the groups are done. Then have everyone gather, and ask each group to perform its commercial for the whole group. Make sure everyone is quiet for each performance—they'll be tempted to talk and put last-minute touches on the commercial while the other groups are performing.

Consider recruiting a couple impartial judges to come to your group and select a winning team. They could use the following criteria for judging: quality of the point made, use of humor, use of the people on the team, and originality. Give a prize to the winning team.

Leave your kids in these teams, as you'll be using them for the next section also.

Make a transition by saying something like—

We're going to discuss a difficult-to-understand picture of God today, that God is like life. Does anyone have any idea what this might mean? Why would God be like life?
Don't work too hard to direct their answers at this point—just solicit a bunch of responses.

There he goes being life again!

Start out this section by asking these questions—

When someone says something or someone is *life-giving*, what do they mean?

That the experience or person added something good to their life.

Which of these things would be life-giving?

☼ **Someone saying something nice about you?**
yes

☼ **Someone giving you a slap on the face?** *no*

☼ **Someone helping you with a problem?** *yes*

☼ **Someone helping you be brave?** *yes*

☼ **Someone ignoring you?** *no*

☼ **Someone giving you an unexpected gift?**
yes

☼ **Someone telling you you're a loser?** *no*

☼ **Someone inviting you to a party?** *yes*

What other kinds of things would be life-giving?

Have kids think of as many answers as possible.

Now make a transition by having everyone turn in their Bibles to John 14:6. Then say something like—

Jesus can be caught *being* life all over in the Bible–encouraging people, giving them direction and hope, and of course, offering salvation. Let's look at a few of those stories.

> **!**
>
> **I** *am the way and the truth and the life. No one comes to the Father except through me.*
> —John 14:6

Keep your kids In the same teams you used for the life commercials. Make sure each team has Bibles (at least one for every two kids). And give them one of the precut slips (they'll be precut because you cut them) from **There He Goes Being Life Again!** (page 26). It would be downright swell if you had an adult in each group also—but I might be dreaming, huh?

If you have fewer than four groups (there are four slips), then just skip one or two. If you have more than four groups, assign the same story to more than one group. Easy!

Tell the teams they should read the passage listed on their slip and then answer the questions written there. Have one person write down the team answers and be prepared to share them with the whole group.

»

A theological thought

A few of you readers who are more theologically inclined are probably having a hissy fit right now—because this lesson is about how God is *like* life. But John 14:6 and many others say Jesus *is* life. Is there a difference? Yes, definitely. For me to say someone (not you, of course) whines like a child does not mean the person *is* a child. The NIV Bible Commentary says, "He *is* the life because he was not subject to death but made it subject to him."

So why is this lesson on how God is like life? First and most pragmatic, is because all 50 of the lessons in *Wild Truth Journal: Pictures of God*, and all 11 other lessons in this book, are built on similes.

Second, and also pragmatic, junior highers are lousy abstract thinkers; and "God is like light" is much easier for them to understand than "God is light."

Finally, it's something of a semantic play—God is like light, and God is light. And while theologically and grammatically there may be a difference, there sure isn't much of a distinction in a 13-year-old mind.

Self-portrait

I'm a lifer!

Hand out copies of **Life-Giving Stuff** (page 27) and pens or pencils to everyone. Allow kids to fill out the questions alone or in pairs. If you prefer, you can easily modify this page to make it a verbal exercise you lead with the entire group. Even if you have kids fill out the sheet first, it's important to debrief it, either in a large group or a small group setting.

This exercise is designed to get kids thinking. There are no right or wrong answers to the case studies. It would be great if kids disagreed a bit and had to defend their rationales.

After discussion and debriefing, if your group is cooperative (the rest of us are jealous of you!), ask kids if they can think of other examples of how a junior higher can be life-like or life-giving.

You'll Need—

- A copy of **Life-Giving Stuff** (page 27)
- Pencils or pens

Print it!

I'm a lifer!

Even if you didn't use the handout on the last exercise, this last section would be best done *with* the handouts. It's good to get kids to write out their own plan of action for applying these character traits.

So pass out copies of **I'm a Lifer!** (page 28) and something to write with, if the kids don't already have it. Give them a couple minutes to come up with a plan of action. Circulate around the room to make sure they understand what they're supposed to be doing. Also, this is an application area where it would be very easy for some kids to really wimp out ("I'm going to smile at my friend this week"). Push them to write a plan of action that takes some courage. That's a little risky. Something like the case studies on page 27.

If your group can handle it, have a few kids (or more) share their action plans. You should listen carefully and be ready to suggest minor changes to make the plans a bit gutsier. Then close in prayer, thanking God for not only being *like* life, but for giving us life! And ask for courage to carry out the plans.

You'll Need—

- A copy of **I'm a Lifer!** (page 28)
- Pencils or pens

Room decoration option

If you're using the wall graphic option described at the end of Lesson 1, add the playing board from the Game of Life (using a real one makes it easy) or a large graphic of the Game of Life's car with those pink and blue stick people in it. Or take it in another direction—use a butterfly.

Dead Man Walking

Read John 11:1-44. Then answer the questions below.

What happened?

How was Jesus like life in this story?

Sand Drawings

Read John 8:1-11. Then answer the questions below.

What happened?

How was Jesus like life in this story?

Muddy Eyes

Read John 9:1-11. Then answer the questions below.

What happened?

How was Jesus like life in this story?

Kid Care

Read Matthew 18:1-6. Then answer the questions below.

What happened?

How was Jesus like life in this story?

Life-Giving Stuff

Which of these are life-giving? (check all that apply)

- ❏ friendship
- ❏ teasing
- ❏ gifts
- ❏ helping
- ❏ cheese-in-a-can

- ❏ encouragement
- ❏ purple jelly beans
- ❏ hugs
- ❏ compliments
- ❏ dung beetles

- ❏ body odor
- ❏ smiles
- ❏ air-sickness bags
- ❏ affirmations
- ❏ defending

Rank these teens in order from the *most* like life (5) to the *least* like life (1)—

_____Roni's friend Sharise seemed depressed all the time recently—and Roni knew it was because Sharise got dumped by her boyfriend last month. So Roni planned a girls' night out for the two of them, and they had a great time. It made Sharise happy.

_____Kevin didn't know Jong—but he knew *about* Jong. Jong got picked on constantly—pushed around in the halls at school, teased, and excluded. Today some of Kevin's friends were throwing little bits of food over at Jong during lunch. Kevin told them all to cut it out. Then he picked up his lunch tray and went to sit with Jong.

_____Leanne's mom has been sad and stressed lately, because Leanne's grandpa is dying. Leanne made a decision to give her mom lots of hugs to try to help her feel better. She's trying to give her mom at least five hugs a day.

_____Richard noticed that one of the janitors at his school always has a big smile on his face and is helpful to everyone. No one really pays much attention to him, of course—he's just there doing his job with a good attitude. So Richard walks up to him and says, "Hey, thanks for putting up with our messes with such a great attitude all the time!"

_____Callie has a teacher—Miss Krasen—who's swamped with work. Miss Krasen is directing the school play and teaching all her classes, and she's got some kind of family crisis that's taking a lot of her time outside of school. Callie wants to help Miss Krasen, so she offers to stay after school for a couple days this week to do whatever Miss Krasen needs. She's not doing it for extra credit or to try to be a teacher's pet—she just wants to help.

WiLDPAGE

i'm a Lifer

Pick one of these life-giving actions—and write out a plan for a way you can put it into action this week. Be specific with your plan! Include the name, day, and place.

- ❏ friendship
- ❏ gifts
- ❏ compliments

- ❏ encouragement
- ❏ hugs
- ❏ affirmations

- ❏ smiles
- ❏ helping
- ❏ other: _____

My life-giving plan—

- -

WiLDPAGE

i'm a Lifer

Pick one of these life-giving actions—and write out a plan for a way you can put it into action this week. Be specific with your plan! Include the name, day, and place.

- ❏ friendship
- ❏ gifts
- ❏ compliments

- ❏ encouragement
- ❏ hugs
- ❏ affirmations

- ❏ smiles
- ❏ helping
- ❏ other: _____

My life-giving plan—

God is like RAiN

He will be like rain falling on a mown lawn, like showers watering the earth. —*Psalm 72:6*

Goals ▶

STUDENTS WILL—

- Understand why God is like rain.
- Talk about how young teens can be like rain.
- Decide how they can be like rain in someone's life.

Picture Prep

Water games for indoors

Play one, two, or all three of these quick games to get started with the idea of water. If your group has five or fewer kids, you can still play the game. Modify it by—

You'll Need—

- Not doing it, but piling the kids into your car and going out for donuts instead!
- Timing your entire group completing the relay as one team, then trying to beat the team's time. *Or,*
- After you explain the activity, having students write down guesses about how long it will take the group to complete the task. Time your group to see whose guess is the closest.

For *Teaspoon Relay Race*—
- teaspoons
- large cups full of water
- small cups (like Dixie cups)

For *Shaving Cream Balloon Squirt* —
- a few trash bags or a plastic drop cloth
- a few balloons
- two cans of shaving cream
- two squirt guns, loaded (with water, of course)

For *Mouthful Relay*—
- large cups of water

Remember, there are three magic syllables that will make this and any curriculum successful for you: *mo-di-fy*! (*Cus-tom-ize* works also; but *Greek-verb-tense* and *suit-and-tie* probably aren't three syllables that will help your lesson much; *glazed do-nuts* might, however!) Okay, back to the plan—

Teaspoon Relay Race
Divide kids into two or more teams. Have each team line up in front of a large cup of water. Place a small empty cup about 15 feet away. Give a teaspoon to the first person in each line. When you give the signal, have the person with the spoon get a spoonful of water from the cup, then walk or run it down to the empty cup, depositing the water there. Each kid then runs back and gives the spoon to the next person in line. This continues until one team has filled its cup.

Shaving Cream Balloon Squirt
Spread some trash bags on the floor, unless you want to be the main character in the new slasher film *Revenge of the Church Janitor.* (Sample lines from the movie trailer: "Look out! He's got a Dustbuster and he's not afraid to use it!" and "What *is* that unmarked jug of red liquid he keeps in his supply closet?").
Anyhow, yeah, you've put down the plastic bags. Now put kids in teams, and have each team choose two representatives to come up front. Give each pair a balloon and some shaving cream. Once they blow up the

balloon, have them cover it with shaving cream as thoroughly as they can. Then give one person in each pair a loaded squirt gun—and have the other person hold the balloon. The pairs race to squirt the shaving cream off their own balloons.

Mouthful Relay

Put your teams in relay formation again. Set a large cup of water in front of each line (the larger, the better), and an empty cup of the same size about 15 feet away. The first people in each line should suck in a mouthful of water (but not swallow it) and run to the empty cup and spit the water into it. Then they run back and tag the next person in line, who does the same thing. The first team to transfer all the water from one cup to the other (or the team with the most water in its cup, if you need them to be extra careful) gets to drink the contents! No—make that they just win.

Water games for outdoors

If your group is meeting at a time and place when you can go outside and play some wetter games, try these.

Water Balloon Toss

Yeah, it's an old one—but it's still a lot of fun. Prepare a bucket full of water balloons. Add water in the bucket (outside the balloons) to keep them wet. This keeps them from breaking when rubbing up against each other. Have kids pair up and stand facing each other, about two feet apart. The pairs should line up across from each other so you end up with two parallel lines.

Give a water balloon to each pair and have them toss it back and forth—once each

way. Then have everyone take one step backward. Kids in each line should stay roughly shoulder-to-shoulder. Now have them toss again, once in each direction. When a pair's balloon breaks, the pair is eliminated. Continue to have remaining pairs toss (their balloons, not their cookies), then take another step back, until you only have one pair remaining.

Trash Can Fill-Up

This is similar to the Teaspoon Relay Race with a few huge differences—it's wetter, it's wilder, and it's not a relay race.

Divide into at least two groups. For each team you'll need a trash can full of water and an empty container of the same size sitting about 30 feet away. It's not essential that the water-filled containers and the empty containers be the same; but it's important that the empty containers all be the same so you can measure a winning team. Give kids a variety of cups. When you give the signal, the free-for-all begins—they have about two minutes to transfer as much water from the full containers to the empty ones as they can. Change the time depending on how fast or slow they're accomplishing their task.

This is not a relay; the whole team can work at the same time. If you have a good relationship with your kids and can get away with it, you (or others) can walk zombie-like through the transfer area and bump into kids, spilling their water. When time is up, measure each trash can to determine the winning team.

Spillage

Give each student a large plastic tumbler filled with water—the bigger, the better. Set some boundaries depending on the size of your group (20 feet by 20 feet for 20 kids). When the game begins, the task is simple—be the last one with water in his cup. You can allow one refilling if you want the game to last a tad longer. (You can allow unlimited refillings if you're not prepared for your lesson and you want this game to last your entire time—not that it's a good idea!)

You'll Need—

For Water Balloon Toss—
- a bucket of water balloons (or trash can, depending on the size of your group)

For Trash Can Fill-Up—
- a bucket full of water (or trash can, depending on the size of your group)
- an empty bucket (or trash can, depending on the size of your group)
- a variety of cups, such as Dixie cups and tumblers (no glass)

For Spillage—
- a large cup or plastic tumbler (the bigger, the better) filled with water for each student
- a small cup (like a Dixie cup)

Action shot

Okay, the games you just played only got the *idea* of water introduced. This lesson, of course (look at the title!) is about *rain*. So you need to make a transition here. Say something like—

Those games involved water, the basic ingredient of rain. And today, we're going to talk about rain.

Then ask these questions—

☺ What are some of the things rain does?
It makes things wet; it brings nourishment to soil and plants; it cleans the air; it sustains life (yeah, like any seventh grader is going to say that!); it refreshes and cools; it makes you ticked that you just washed your car.

☺ Why is rain a good thing?
This is fairly obvious, and the answers should be contained in the answers to the last question. But it will clarify your point.

☺ How can people *be* like rain?
This will be a tough question for some of your kids—specifically, those who are still operating primarily with concrete thinking. That people can be like rain is a very abstract idea. It should be interesting to see what your students come up with on this puppy! It's okay if they still don't completely understand the idea, because you'll flesh it out more in the next exercise.

Rain memory

Make the transition by explaining that, just as in all the lessons in this series, you and the group are going to see how this character trait is part of who God is—that they all are self-portraits he shows us in the Bible so we can understand who he is. Ask—

☺ How is God like rain?

☺ Why would God use this picture to describe himself? What do you think he wants us to see or understand?

☺ What difference can it make for you and me that God is like rain?

Now show the group Hosea 6:3 (you also can show them Psalm 72:6, written out at the beginning of this lesson, if you'd like).

Tell the kids you'd like to memorize this verse together—to get the God-is-like-rain idea stuck in their heads a bit. But you're going to use motions to help remember the verse. Have everyone stand up and say the verse with you, while you show them the motions. Make up your own motions or use these—

You'll Need—

☺ Hosea 6:3 on an overhead.

> **L**et us acknowledge the LORD; let us press on to acknowledge him. As surely as the sun rises, he will appear; he will come to us like the winter rains, like the spring rains that water the earth.
> —Hosea 6:3

Acknowledge	point to your own head
the Lord	point up
press on	fighter's stance (fists up)
acknowledge him	point to your own head and then up
surely	slap fist into open hand
the sun rises	hands and arms in arch rise above head
will appear	arms outstretched
come to us	beckoning motion ("come here") with hand
winter	hug yourself and shiver

rains	descending hands with wiggling fingers (you know, the universal rain symbol)
the spring	palms up, hands circle out away from body
rains	uh, the URS (universal rain symbol) again
the earth	of course, the UES (universal earth symbol), also known as the UROS (universal round object symbol)—draw a circle in the air with your hands

Review the verse with motions several times, increasing your speed a bit each time. Then remove the overhead transparency (or whatever you're using) and do it a couple more times. Ask sections of your group or individual students to try it.

Self-portrait

Rainy-day teens

You'll Need—

- ꙮ A sign that says TOTALLY LIKE RAIN
- ꙮ A sign that says NOT ONE BIT LIKE RAIN

Place a sign that says TOTALLY LIKE RAIN on one wall and a sign that says NOT ONE BIT LIKE RAIN on the opposite wall. Explain to your students you've created a continuum, like a big scale across the room, with NOT ONE BIT LIKE RAIN equaling one and TOTALLY LIKE RAIN equaling 10. When you read a short description of a student who may or may not be *rain-like*, they need to stand somewhere between the two signs to show how rain-like they think the character is. Have your kids stand up, and start reading. After students have decided where to stand, ask, "How was this student like rain?" to check for understanding.

ꙮ **Sabrina noticed that her dad was a bit gloomy after a long day at work, so she made him a hot cup of cappuccino.**

ꙮ **Paul realized Justin has absolutely no friends, so he invited him to a youth group party.**

ꙮ **Claire stepped in and helped cool down an argument between two friends.**

ꙮ **Max sprayed his sister with the garden hose.**

ꙮ **Tasha encouraged her teacher by telling her how good class was today.**

ꙮ **Patrick stops by a retirement home every Tuesday to visit an old guy with no family.**

ꙮ **Logan sat with a kid at lunch who usually sits by himself.**

ꙮ **Mary tries to smile and say hi to people that others ignore.**

Ask—

Which one of these kids were the most like rain? Why?

Have your teens brainstorm a bit on ways *junior highers* can be like rain. If you ever use small groups (please tell me you do!), this would be a great question to talk about in that context—it's much easier for junior highers to talk in the third person (he should do this, she should do that) than it is for them to talk in first person (I would do this or that).

Print it!

Be the rain

Can you believe it? You're at the end of a lesson without doing a single reproducible handout! Of course, as always, if your group thinks handouts cause leprosy, you could modify this exercise into a small group discussion fairly easily (although having kids actually write out an application step sure helps to solidify any speck of learning that took place today).

You'll see that **Be the Rain** (page 34) has two sections. The first has two case studies asking your students to suggest how this teen can be like rain. The second section asks kids to think of a situation in their own lives where they could be like rain.

Remember, this is not an easy conceptual leap for concrete thinkers. Don't be surprised if kids write things, in earnest, like—"I can water my mom's plants" or "I can wash my dad's car." Some will still not quite get that you haven't been talking about literal rain or

You'll Need—

- ○ Copies of **Be the Rain** (page 34)
- ○ Pens or pencils

water for the past 45 minutes. Ah, the pain/joy/torture/thrill of teaching young teens! Take a few minutes to either—

- Have kids fill out the first section on their own, then discuss their answers.

- Or do the first section together, without having kids actually write anything. This would, by the way, also be a great small group activity.

Finally, ask students to write out a situation in their lives right now where they could be a cooling effect in an overheated situation, bring refreshment to a dry situation (of course, some kid will write, "I can bring a Coke to..."), or bring strength and encouragement to the weak. After all the kids have written something, have them share their answers with someone—either with the whole group if your group is small enough or in small groups if your group is large.

Be sure to close in prayer, thanking God for being like rain in our lives and asking God to help us be like rain for other people.

Room decoration option

If you're using the big-ol'-picture-on-the-wall idea described at the end of Lesson 1, you can add a cloud with a bunch of rain coming out of it or just one giant water droplet.

Be the Rain

Roberto works an after-school job a couple days a week at a gas station. He pretty much just does whatever needs to be done that no one else wants to do—washing rags and picking up trash in the shop area, pumping gas at the full-service island, stocking the snacks. Everyone else who works at the station is really grumpy—all the time. They're always complaining about how much their job stinks and about how lousy their lives are. Roberto figures he has as much right to complain as anyone, considering that he does the worst work. For a while he joins in the crabby attitude. But lately he's been thinking he'd like to be like rain in this place. What are some of the things you think he could do?

Sara's home is a bit tense. Her stepdad works really long hours, partly because he's a workaholic, and partly because his job is really demanding. Her mom works a lot too, but she's also dealing with stress about her aging mother (Sara's grandma). Sara's older brother Steve is trying to decide which college to go to, whether or not to break up with his girlfriend, and how to finish his senior year without going crazy, because he's sick of school. Most days, Sara would rather just hide in her room and listen to CDs or talk on the phone. But she wants to be like rain for her family. What are some things you think she could do?

Write about a situation in your life where you could be like rain. When and where and how–exactly–will you do this rainy stuff?

God is like a LAMB

The next day John saw Jesus coming toward him and said, "Look, the Lamb of God, who takes away the sin of the world!" —*John 1:29*

Goals

STUDENTS WILL—

- Understand the theological concept of Jesus as the Lamb, the sacrifice offered for our sins.
- List ways young teens can sacrifice.
- Make a plan to be lamb-like.

Picture Prep

Lamb-o-rama

Pass out copies of **Lamb-o-rama** (page 40) and writing utensils. Read through the instructions and items out loud so that all your kids are clear on what they're supposed to do. They can complete the items in any order they wish but can only get a person's initials one time (if your group is small, you may have to modify this last rule). Give the starting signal and let 'em go at it. It would be great if you could play some rowdy background music while they're frenetically filling out their sheets.

Award a prize of some sort to the first teen finished—a candy bar is fine, but I've found strange canned goods to be lots of fun. Nothing like a can of octopus or sauerkraut juice to put some random zip

You'll Need—

- 🐑 Copies of **Lamb-o-rama** (page 40)
- 🐑 Pens or pencils
- 🐑 A clip of sheep from the movie *Babe* (optional)
- 🐑 TV and VCR (optional)

in your meeting time!

It would be fun to show a clip from the movie *Babe*. There are some great scenes with sheep (close enough to lambs, right?)—talking sheep, no less—that would give your kids a mutton-visual.

Action shot

Sacrifice talk and discussion

It's time for some pretty heavy-duty theology (buck up!). This may be very familiar to some of you amazing junior high workers (you are so cool for working with young teens). But in case it's not, let me give you a bit-o-background info.

In the Old Testament, under the old covenant, God required sacrifices to atone for sin. The priests would offer these on

You'll Need—

- 🐑 Bibles
- 🐑 A short prepared talk (see outline)
- 🐑 Pictures of sheep (optional, see text directions)
- 🐑 Blank paper
- 🐑 Pens or pencils
- 🐑 CD and CD player (optional)

behalf of the people following very clear guidelines set forth in the Law. Lots of animals were used for sacrifices—depending on the situation—but an unblemished lamb was commonly used. Some Old Testament writers told of a sacrifice to come that would take away all the sins of the world. Of course, God brought the new covenant about through the sacrificial work of Jesus on the cross. In his death, Jesus became the end-all sacrifice for all sin. And as such, Jesus is often referred to in the Bible as *the Lamb*. Your kids will need to gain a basic working knowledge of this idea in order to understand this lesson.

Make a transition with these questions—

ö **What were lambs used for in the Old Testament, other than the things lambs are normally used for, such as food and wool?**

ö **In the Bible, John sees Jesus approaching and says, "Look, the Lamb of God, who takes away the sin of the world!" Why do you think John would say that? Why is Jesus referred to as the Lamb?**

ö **Why do you think they call Jesus *the* Lamb, instead of just *a* Lamb?**

Now, give a short (three- to five-minute) talk summarizing the theology described in the opening paragraph in this section.

If there's any way you can have photos of sheep and lambs showing on a screen while you're talking, it will add a great visual edge to your message, though this is a major prep step for most people. If you use PowerPoint, you can find shots of sheep on the Internet and paste them into a slide show.

If you want, you can use these main points—

ö **Because God is perfect, there's a price to be paid for sin. In the Old Testament, this was done with animal sacrifices.**
Warning! Some kids will get hung up here. Their compassion for kitties and puppies will make the idea of animal sacrifices wholly unacceptable.

Gauge their response, because it would be better not to get sidetracked here—but if you need to, explain that the OT culture had a completely different view of animals than people do today, and this was not considered gross or mean at all.

ö **Lambs were pretty commonly used for sacrifices.**

ö **When Jesus died on the cross for our sins, he became the last sacrifice for sin ever needed. We can experience God's forgiveness because of Jesus' sacrifice.**

ö **That's why Jesus is called the Lamb. He's the only one needed now.**

Have everyone turn to Revelation 5:12. Say something like—

I want to show you a little future scene from heaven. Everyone is gathered around Jesus, and they're singing the words in this verse, "Worthy is the Lamb, who was slain, to receive power and wealth and wisdom and strength and honor and glory and praise!"

Use these questions, or others you come up with, to discuss the idea of Jesus as a lamb—

ö **Why would the singers in that verse say Jesus is worthy to receive honor and glory and all that other stuff? What's that mean?**
It means that Jesus deserves all those things, because of the role he played in paying for all our sins.

ö **What's the verse mean when it says the Lamb was slain?**
This is a total repeat of things you've already talked about—you're just checking for understanding.

⚙ What difference does it make that Jesus was slain for us?

It's the only way we can have forgiveness of our sins, relationship with God, and entrance into heaven—pretty major stuff!

⚙ Does this picture of God help you understand him in any new ways? How?

God is giving; he gives to the point of sacrificing his own son in order to reach out to us.

⚙ If you were standing outside the temple in the Old Testament, and the priest was going through the process of sacrificing a lamb so that you could have forgiveness for your sins, what would you be thinking?

You'll get a wide variety of responses—anywhere from "I'd be thankful" to "I'd be grossed out" to "I'd wanna jump up there and rescue the sheep." Don't look for a right answer here.

Now pass out blank paper, and make sure kids still have something to write with from the opening exercise (some of your guys may have systematically destroyed their writing utensils by now). It would be best if you had some mellow music playing in the background to help kids from being distracted by one another. Then continue—

Close your eyes and picture yourself standing by the cross, as Jesus is being sacrificed. In your mind, look around at the other people by the cross. Look up at Jesus. Think about the fact that this Lamb is being sacrificed so you can experience forgiveness, heaven, and a relationship with God. Now take a minute to write your thoughts on paper. What would you be thinking at that moment? What would you want to say to Jesus? What difference does it make, really, that he's up there on the cross in the first place? Write these thoughts down on your papers.

After you've finished (you'll probably need to give the kids about two or three minutes), ask if a few students would be willing to read their thoughts to the whole group. If you're using small groups, have kids share in that context.

Self-portrait

Big transition to make here! This self-portrait of God's character translates to our character a bit differently than many of the others. It's fairly obvious really, that you won't be suggesting your kids literally sacrifice themselves on behalf of someone else—what kind of freaky curriculum do you think this is? On top of the fact that you just might get into trouble (read: you'll spend the rest of your life in prison!), your kids would be powerless to save anyone. But we can sacrifice *for* people. We can put their needs before our own and give up things to benefit other people. That's where we're going here, okay?

Teen lambs

Make a transitional joke by saying something like—

Now, I want you all to think of a way that you can die for someone this week...just kidding!

Toss out this question, without fishing for a *right* answer—

Really, we're not going to suggest that God wants us to get slaughtered. But we should be able to develop in ourselves the characteristic of sacrificing. What would it look like for a teenager to sacrifice for someone else?

Some of your older kids might be able to answer this, especially if they understand the more common use of the word sacrifice (meaning, to give up instead of to kill!).

Now ask five volunteers to come to the front of the room. Put a nametag or sign on each of them with the names CORA, OLIVIA, HENRY, JIN, and JUAN (Jin is a girl, by the way). Tell your kids you're going to read five stories of sacrifice and afterward you're going to ask the group to position the five in order of least to most lamb-like. Have the appropriate nametag wearer step forward when you read his or her story.

You'll Need—

- Five volunteers—three girls, two boys
- Large nametags or signs to hang around their necks labeled CORA, OLIVIA, HENRY, JIN, and JUAN

Cora's grandma has been putting together a bunch of scrapbooks about her life. But last month, Cora's grandma had a stroke, so she can't do the work anymore. Cora decided to give up her gymnastics lessons, something she really loves, so she can go to her grandma's after school three days a week and help with the scrapbooks.

Olivia's group of friends decided to get together Friday night, but they couldn't agree on what to do. Olivia really wanted to go to the mall, but most the other girls wanted to rent a video. Olivia didn't really care about seeing a video but told her friends she'd be happy to do whatever they wanted.

Henry is totally into a certain band. Their lyrics aren't super bad or anything, but they're not Christian either. Henry's friend Luke is a new Christian and can't understand why Henry would even listen to that band. It really bothers Luke. Henry decides that he'll stop listening to the band so that he won't cause a problem for Luke's faith.

The only money Jin makes is from a weekly two-hour babysitting job. That money is all she has for going out with friends or buying things. But Jin decided to pitch in with a couple friends and sponsor a poor kid in Africa. It's taking more than half of her money every week.

Juan has a tough choice to make. His little brother, Jesus, wants Juan to come to his soccer tournament this weekend, but Juan's been invited to spend the weekend with a friend. He really doesn't care much about seeing his brother's tournament, but he knows it will mean so much to Jesus if he goes. Juan decides to go to the tournament.

After reading the stories, mention that all of them are good examples of lamb-like sacrifice—the characters gave something up for someone else. In a very, very small way, this is similar to Jesus giving up his life for us. Ask your kids which character was the most lamb-like. Move the five volunteers around to put them in order as the group directs you. You might need to remind them of the stories with phrases like "Olivia didn't push her choice of the mall on her friends," or "Jin's giving up her money to sponsor a kid in Africa." Make this very interactive and verbal. Encourage debate. And make it *fun!*

End this section by asking—

What are some other ways that teens can be lamb-like?

Print it!

I say baa!

Pass out copies of **I Say Baa!** (page 41). This exercise, as usual, could be easily modified and done without the handouts, if you prefer (though I really like making kids write down their application plans—it acts as a thickening agent to solidify their thinking and action).

The sheet is fairly self-explanatory—kids need to write about a time when they *were* lamb-like and then write about a way they can do this in the next week or two. As usual, you'll want to have them do the first section first

You'll Need—

- 🐑 Copies of **I Say Baa!** (page 41)
- 🐑 Pins to prick fingers so kids have something fresh to write with. Oops! Make that pens or pencils

(duh!), discuss and debrief, then, move on to the second section, followed by discussion, sharing, and debriefing.

This would be a great lesson to consider some sort of collective response. How can your whole group sacrifice something together for someone or a group of people? Maybe you can be like Jin and sponsor a kid together. Or maybe everyone could donate a sleeping bag or blanket to a homeless shelter. Allow them to brainstorm an idea they can get behind and *own.*

Then end with prayer.

Yes, all the lessons end with a suggestion for prayer. This isn't just because it's "how we do things." It's to refocus on God, instead of on us. But for this lesson especially, it's great to spend time in prayer thanking Jesus for his truly amazing lamb-work on the cross. Truly, this is the basis of everything we are and the hope we have.

Room decoration option

If you're using the wall graphic option described in Lesson 1, stick a big drawing of a lamb on your wall (that one was pretty obvious, huh?).

Lamb-o-rama

Complete these items in any order you want, but only get the initials of each person once.

Shearing Time

Lambs and sheep often get their coats shaved off. Find someone who's willing to pull out a strand of his or her own hair and give it to you.

Have that person initial here: _____

Mary's Tune

Get in a group with two other people and sing "Mary Had a Little Lamb" as loud as you can.

Have them both initial here: _____ _____

Counting Sheep

Sometimes when people can't sleep, they count imaginary sheep jumping over a fence. Act like a fence and have someone jump over you.

Have that person initial here: _____

Bleating Chorus

Get with two other people and sing "Mary Had a Little Lamb" in sheep voices (it's called bleating—you know, baa-baa).

Have them initial here: _____ _____

Bo-Peep

Stand on a chair and yell, "Where are my sheep?" When you can find someone willing to be your lost sheep, have them come over to you.

Have that person initial here: _____

¡ Say Baa!

I have said, "Baa!"

Describe a time when you sacrificed something for someone else—

How difficult was it? Mark an **X** on the line to show your answer.

●——————————————————————————————————●

no big deal   it wasn't easy   it felt like a sacrifice   it was big-time hard!

What was the result?

I will say, "Baa!"

How can you be lamb-like by sacrificing something for someone in the next couple weeks? Be specific—name the person and situation, what you'll sacrifice, and when you'll do it.

One final hard question—why should you sacrifice for others?

(41)

God is like a DAD

How great is the love the Father has lavished on us, that we should be called children of God! And that is what we are! —1 John 3:1

Goals

STUDENTS WILL—

- Understand that the *God is like a Father* picture speaks of his unconditional love.
- Examine the difference between conditional and unconditional expressions of love.
- Reflect on a recent experience with conditional love, and make a plan to show unconditional love to someone this week.

Picture Prep

Famous dads

Divide your group into teams for this relatively quiet game. The size of the teams isn't important—perhaps group of six to 12, but even as small as two each will work. You can have as many teams as you want but it's a good idea to have an adult leader in each team to keep the kids honest.

Once kids are in their teams, explain that you're going to give them a series of clues to a famous dad. You'll give three clues, and you'll pause after each clue for the team to talk and to come up with an answer. Of course, they don't want the other teams to hear their discussion, but you don't have to tell them that.

If they have a guess, they should write it down. They can change it after getting more clues if they want. Tell your students there are no trick answers—for instance, males they

didn't know were dads. Every correct answer is someone who has children whom they should know.

When you reveal the answers, they'll get—

- 100 points for every famous dad they guess correctly after the first clue.
- 50 points for every famous dad they guess correctly after the second clue.
- 25 points for every famous dad they guess correctly after the third clue.

Now if your kids are anything like the average young teen, some will want to cheat and say they had the answer after an early round when they really didn't get it on their papers until a later round. That's why I'm suggesting you have an adult in each group. The adults can't help give answers—they're only there to guide!

After reading all the clues for one dad, ask who the famous dad is. Reveal the correct answer, awarding points before moving on to the next round. By the way, you don't have to play all the rounds—just use as many as you have time for.

Round 1

1. I'm in the Bible. In fact, I'm in the Old Testament. And I wasn't a very happy guy. But I was a king.

You'll Need—

- Blank piece of paper
- Pens or pencils
- An adult for each team

2. I really struggled with jealousy. In fact, it just about drove me crazy when women sang about me killing thousands, but some other guy killing ten thousands.

3. I tried to kill my son's best friend, David. I chucked my spear at him. I hunted him. But he eventually became king.

Answer: Saul, father of Jonathan.

Round 2

1. Hi, I'm on TV! Woo-hoo!

2. I work at a nuclear power plant. I really, really like donuts.

3. I have no hair, and my face is kind of yellow-orange, 'cause I'm a cartoon. I'm famous for mess-ups and for saying, "Doh!"

Answer: Homer Simpson, from the TV show "The Simpsons."

Round 3

1. I was on TV back in the 1970s, but you've seen me on reruns.

2. I'm a pretty groovy dad, and I have three girls and three boys.

3. We're a blended family—the girls were with their mom when I married her.

Answer: Mike Brady (Mr. Brady would be okay), from the TV show "The Brady Bunch."

Round 4

1. I'm a politician, or at least, I was.

2. In fact, I was the president of the United States!

3. My daughter Chelsea was a teenager when I became president.

Answer: Bill Clinton.

Round 5

1. Yup, I'm another Bible dad, but I'm in the New Testament.

2. I was more of a stepdad. I mean, I was there when my son was born, but he's not officially my birth son.

3. I was a carpenter.

Answer: Joseph, earthly father of Jesus

Round 6

1. I'm royalty, and you're not!
2. I have two boys: William and Harry
3. I might become the king of England.

Answer: Prince Charles

Bjorn's wild days

Recruit a handful of volunteer actors to be a part of a spontaneous melodrama. These kids don't have to prepare any parts; they'll just respond to the script as it's read. If they have any lines, they just repeat them, in character, after you read them.

The best qualification for a good spontaneous melodrama actor is not acting ability, it's hamminess. They probably won't have a clue what you're talking about, but, since the drama takes place in Norway, they should try to use Norwegian sing-songy accents.

You'll Need—

- A copy of **Bjorn's Wild Days** (page 47)
- Volunteer actors
- Bibles

Everyone who's been in church more than three days will recognize this drama as a twist on the Parable of the Lost Son (or the Prodigal Son). So, without further ado, once you're finished with the Broadway-quality drama and have profusely thanked your acting team, have students turn in their Bibles to Luke 15:11-32. Read the story out loud.

Say something like—

This is one of the longer pictures of God in the Bible

—almost a movie script! Jesus gives us this picture story to help us catch a glimpse of God.

Then ask—

🐾 **What kind of father is the one in the story?**

Your kids will probably answer, "a good one," and you'll want to drop-kick them. Push them for a deeper answer.

🐾 **What did the father do to prove his love?**

He accepted the son back without an apology or an explanation for his actions. The father's love was obviously unconditional—without conditions.

🐾 **What did the son do to deserve the father's love?**

Not a thing!

🐾 **Why do we have such a hard time believing that God's love has no strings attached, like this story shows?**

This is a difficult question—one you might even wrestle with yourself. The answer revolves around the fact that we have so few earthly examples of true unconditional love. Most people, even those who love us the most, usually attach, at least occasionally, some amount of condition to their love: "I love you if…" or "I love you when…" Explain that conditional love is love that has conditions attached to it—you have to do something or be a certain way to get it.

Self-portrait

Show some daddy-love!

Stick two simple signs on your walls (unless you're, like, meeting in a forest—then, I suppose you'll have to stick them on trees or some-thing). Point these signs out to your kids. Then read the following just-made-up, but real-life examples, and have your kids stand by the CONDITIONAL sign, the UNCONDITIONAL sign, or somewhere in between to register how conditional or unconditional they think the person's love is.

Jesse's sister needs help with her homework. Jesse says, "I'll help you if you do my chores this week."

Kim writes an encouraging note to a friend, and sends it anonymously, because she doesn't want her friend to feel like she has to thank Kim.

Tony gives his dessert to Nathan. Nathan doesn't have a dessert, and Tony's trying to be cool to him; but he also hopes that Nathan will think he's a wonderful person for doing this.

Sharon would love to be noticed by Rachel, a really popular girl. When Rachel asks Sharon for help studying for a science test, Sharon is happy to help. She knows this is her chance to be accepted into the popular kids' group.

Before you move to the next section, you're going to need to address this tough issue: many people have a hard time seeing the "God is like a Father" thing as good, because they don't have a good example of a father here on earth. Some of your kids don't have dads. Or they may have been abused by their dads or stepdads. Many won't feel close to their dads. Mention this, and say that the picture God gives us of himself here is one of a perfect father—the father of everyone's dreams. And the main characteristic of this picture is unconditional love.

Chaz wants to help his mom, who's been working too hard these days. So he offers to wash the dishes all week, even though he's only supposed to do it one time.

Carly's friend Amber told a mean lie about her. It really hurt Carly. But she chose to forgive Amber and not hold a grudge against her.

Now, have your kids give advice to these two characters—

Gina is really frustrated. Her friend Kayla blew her off and started hanging out with a really popular crowd. Kayla even made fun of Gina in the halls when she was with these new friends. Then the group rejected Kayla. And now Kayla wants to be all buddy-buddy with Gina again. Gina's not sure she can trust Kayla, and she's still pretty hurt.

👁 **How can Gina show unconditional daddy-love to Kayla?**

👁 **What should she do?**

👁 **What would you do?**

Fernando doesn't know what to do. His dad keeps making excuses why he can't play basketball with Fernando when he said he would. It's happened three times in the last week. Fernando feels like saying, "Fine, I'll ignore you until you follow through on your promise!" But he doesn't really know what to do.

👁 **How can Fernando show unconditional daddy-love to his own father?**

👁 **What should he do?**

👁 **What would you do?**

Print it!

Last week/next week

Pass out half-sheet copies of **Last Week/Next Week** (page 48) and pens or pencils to each student. Then ask them to take a minute and think back on this last week. Tell them to write down a time when they showed conditional love to someone. They don't have to write the whole story— just enough to jog their memory. If you're using small groups—or if you *are* a small group—this would be good to debrief. But it's probably too much to expect kids to share this kind of thing in a large group setting.

Then spend some time in prayer thanking God for his unconditional love for us. Ask him for help in showing that same kind of love to others—without expecting anything in return.

After you pray, ask kids to think of a person who needs a dose of *un*conditional love this week. Maybe it's a friend; maybe a parent or sibling. Tell them to write a plan for how they will do this without making it be conditional. Have a few kids share their plans, especially in a small group context.

You'll Need—

👁 Half-sheet copies of **Last Week/Next Week** (page 48)
👁 Pens or pencils

Room decoration option

If you're using the wall graphic option described in Lesson 1, add a large graphic of a dad—say, a man wearing a tie. You might want to put a big red heart on his chest to signify unconditional love.

Bjorn's Wild Days

A spontaneous melodrama based on the Parable of the Lost Son in Luke 15:11-32.

Characters

Bjorn
2 to 4 polar bears

Bjorn's father
2 to 4 ice sculptors

One cold Norwegian day, Bjorn walked out to his father's ice-fishing hut. It was really cold, and both of them kept shivering and stamping their feet to stay warm. Bjorn said,

"Hey, Father! Have ya caught any fish?"

"Ya, Bjorn," answered the father, "They're really bitin' this morning."

Bjorn was nervous, and added to his shivering from being cold, he starting shaking so hard he looked like he was having a seizure! Finally, his father walked over, smacked him on the arm and said, "What is it, boy?" Bjorn said, "Father, I want you to give me the fish farm money you saved for me. I'm going to try livin' with the wild ice sculptors for a while."

Bjorn's father was not very excited about this, but gave Bjorn the money anyhow; and off went Bjorn, still shaking out of control.

Bjorn moved in with the wild ice sculptors and they had cold and wild parties, as you would imagine. They danced. In fact, they danced wildly. *Wildly!* They drank a lot too, and they all ended up falling down drunk. They would get back up and dance some more, then fall down again. This happened over and over again.

Eventually the wild ice sculptors went away, because Bjorn was out of money and couldn't pay for their parties. He said, "Oh no, I'm out of money!"

Then Bjorn got a job feeding polar bears. It was a tough job because the polar bears were kind of rough with Bjorn. They'd push him around and roar at him. It scared him, and he started shaking again! But when the polar bears curled up to sleep, Bjorn was so hungry, he was tempted to eat the stinky little fish he fed them. He picked a fish up and held it to his nose—but the smell was so bad Bjorn threw up all over the polar bears.

Bjorn decided to go home. Even the entry-level fish cleaners at his father's fish farm had a better life than he did. So off he went in the direction of home.

When he was still a long ways from home, his father, who was ice fishing again, saw Bjorn. He ran to him like a madman, screaming, "Bjorn, Bjorn, Bjorn!" He hugged Bjorn and lifted him off the ground. Bjorn was confused and said, "I'm confused!"

And his father said, "My cold little boy was lost, and now he's found. That warms me up!"

Bjorn's father threw a big party to honor Bjorn. The polar bears and the wild ice sculptors all came, and they had a great time!

WILDPAGE

Last Week/Next Week

A time I used conditional love this past week

When, how, and to whom I'll show *unconditional* love this coming week

---
✂ -

WILDPAGE

Last Week/Next Week

A time I used conditional love this past week

When, how, and to whom I'll show *unconditional* love this coming week

God is like BREAD

I am the bread of life. —*John 6:48*

Goals

STUDENTS WILL—

- Grasp why Jesus is like bread (or how anyone can be like bread), a difficult simile.
- Learn to identify *hunger* in people.
- Make a plan for being bread-like this week.

Picture Prep

Depending on the creativity, rambunctiousness and willingness of your students, pick either Bread Sculptures or Bread Wars as your opening exercise—

Bread sculptures

Divide your group into teams of three or four (you can use larger teams—say, eight or nine—if your group is really large). Give each team a pile of toothpicks and a loaf of cheap bread, and ask them to make a sculpture. Give them no more guidance, and then tell them they have three minutes and have them begin. You can judge the sculptures at the end and award a candy prize to the team that wins.

Consider using one of these variations from the beginning or as a Round 2—

You'll Need—

- Loaves of bread (at least one per team)
- Toothpicks (about half a box per team)

- *Themed sculptures*—Ask the teams to construct a sculpture that represents something they've learned in the last couple weeks in your group.

- *Rapid-fire themes*—Give teams one minute to create a sculpture based on a theme or word you give them. Quickly judge them, then move onto another theme or word. Use four or five in a row.

- *Heigh-ho sculptures*—With this variation, art doesn't matter—just height. Which team can create the tallest sculpture in two minutes?

Bread wars

This is, admittedly, not amazingly creative—but it's a lot of fun and gets kids handling bread (a tangible experience with bread will help your lesson). It's basically dodge ball with bread! Yeah, this is youth ministry at its finest, huh?

Divide your group into two teams and place them on two sides of a playing area (or use more than two teams and only have two compete at one time). Give each team several loaves of bread (depending on the size of your group). There are two ways you can play this silly game:

- For milder indoor play, tell your students they are not allowed to wad up the bread. They have to throw the slices like a Frisbee. Anyone who gets hit by bread is out. Anyone who catches a piece of bread gets the thrower out.

For wilder indoor or outdoor play, don't tell them what they can or can't do with the bread. Just tell them how they get out. After a short time, kids will figure out that if they squish the bread into a ball they can do much more damage!

You'll Need—

- A large playing area like a gym or a field
- Several loaves of bread for each team

If you play the game indoors, you have the wonderful opportunity to create years of tension between you and the church custodian! (You're thinking, "As if that doesn't already exist!") If you play the game outdoors, you'll be tempted to leave the bread pieces for the critters to pick up—and get all the naturalists upset with you. Your choice.

Jesus–bread of life

Pass out copies of **Jesus—Bread of Life** (page 53) and pens or pencils to each wonderful, respectful, polite teen—well, to that one, and then to all the others also. Ask them to work in twos or threes to complete the sheet.

The worksheet, as you can see, starts with a list of things bread does and doesn't do. Most of them (all but two) are things that bread does. But only two of them ("satisfies your hunger," and "fills you up") are connected to the God-is-like-bread picture. The bottom line here is that God fulfills our longings—our hungers. You'll also see on the sheet that your kids will try to spot Jesus being like bread in three passages. In each of these, he fulfills someone's

You'll Need—

- Copies of **Jesus—Bread of Life** (page 53)
- Pens or pencils
- Bibles

hunger for something. And your kids will be asked to identify what that hunger was. This is the bottom-line skill you're hoping they will learn as a result of this lesson—to identify the hunger their friends have and then try to fill 'em up! You'll clarify this in the third step of this lesson.

Oh, and by the way, be aware that this is majorly abstract stuff. It will be difficult for some of your younger kids to get their concrete-thinking brains around the idea that a person can be *like* bread. You may have to help them across the bridge by saying something like, "Okay, if Jesus is like bread because he takes away our hunger, that doesn't mean our hunger for food. What kinds of things do people hunger for, besides food, that Jesus can give them?"

With this kind of exercise, it would be great to play some cool music while the students are completing their work. When your students seem to be done with the sheet—maybe eight minutes—take some time to debrief it. Ask which of the list of bread-like qualities apply to Jesus and how. Ask what they discovered about how Jesus is like bread in the individual passages.

If you'd rather, you could easily convert this section into a 10-minute talk, using the passages on the Wildpage.

Bready teens

Ask—

- **What's the basic issue with this bread thing? In other words, when God says he's like bread, what does it mean?**

You'll Need—

- Whiteboard and markers (optional)

He meets our needs completely, he satisfies our hungers completely.

◌ **What does it mean for people to hunger for things other than food?**
They really want or need that thing.

◌ **What kinds of things do other teens you know hunger for?**
Spend some time on this one—maybe even creating a list on a board. Things like acceptance, love, friendship, fun, a good relationship with their parents, to succeed at something.

◌ **How can Jesus satisfy those hungers?**
Jesus wants to meet all our needs. And he does this in a variety of ways: by bringing people into our lives to meet those needs, by meeting the needs directly himself, by taking away the hunger, and even sometimes by allowing us to experience hunger in a way that draws us closer to him—the ultimate hunger!

◌ **How can teenagers be bread-like?**
By looking for areas where people are hungry and trying to meet those needs.

Read these case studies to your group, and then ask them to tell you how the main character was like bread—

Amy loves lunchtime at school because it's the one time in her day when she gets to hang out with her friends. But lately it's been bugging her that she keeps noticing this girl named Kate. Kate is always sitting by herself. So Amy decides to talk to Kate one day. Then the next day, after she's gotten to know Kate a little bit, Amy invites Kate to come sit with her and her friends.

◌ **How's Kate hungry?**
She's hungry for friends.

◌ **How was Anna like bread?**
She filled up Kate's hunger for someone to sit with at lunch.

Jeremy has this old guy that lives two houses away from him named Mr. Bernstein. Mr. Bernstein's wife died about five years ago, and his grown children live in other states. He seems like a really lonely guy, but he's always been friendly to Jeremy. Jeremy knows Mr. Bernstein is good at chess, so Jeremy asks Mr. Bernstein to teach him. Jeremy is happy to learn how to play chess but really just wants to hang out once in a while with Mr. Bernstein.

◌ **How was Mr. Bernstein hungry?**
He was hungry for someone to talk to, for companionship.

◌ **How was Jeremy like bread?**
He filled up Mr. Bernstein's loneliness.

Paige's friend Natalie struggles in math. She just doesn't get it; and she gets pretty bad grades in math class. Natalie's parents are always on her case about her math grades, which totally stresses her out. Paige is pretty good at math. She figures she can help Natalie get better grades and reduce the stress of her parents being hacked all the time. So Paige starts unofficially tutoring Natalie. The two of them look over Natalie's homework every morning, and Paige helps her understand where she went wrong.

◌ **How was Natalie hungry?**
She was hungry for better grades, and hungry to reduce the stress of having her parents upset about her grades.

◌ **How was Paige like bread?**

She filled up Natalie's need to understand math, and in doing so, reduced the stress between Natalie and her parents.

If you have time, divide your students into groups and have them create short dramas showing a teen being like bread. This will force them to apply the concept more, as they'll have to think up a scenario on their own about what this simile means.

Print it!

Hi, I'm bread

This is a pretty straightforward application here, since your students should totally understand the point of this lesson by now. Pass out copies of **Hi, I'm Bread** (page 54) to your kids. They should still have pens or pencils from **Jesus—Bread of Life**.

Ask your group to think quietly for a minute, asking God who they know that's hungry in some way. If your group is young and has struggled with the abstract nature of this simile, you might want to add something like—

Remember, we're not talking about someone who's hungry for food here—we're talking about people who are hungry in other ways.

After they've thought about someone who's hungry, they should describe the person's hunger and come up with a bread-plan on their paper. Play some music in the background while they're working on this so it's not totally silent in your room (right, like it's ever totally silent!).

After a few minutes, have a few students share their plans. Or better yet, have your group break up into small groups with an adult in each one, and have kids and adults share their plans with their small group.

You'll Need—

- Copies of **Hi, I'm Bread** (page 54)
- Pens or pencils
- CD and CD player

Room decoration option
If you're using the room decoration idea described at the end of lesson one, add a large graphic of a loaf of bread to your wall.

Jesus—Bread of Life

Which of the following things does bread do? (Check all that apply)

- ❏ satisfies your hunger
- ❏ competes in Olympic bobsledding
- ❏ sops things up from your plate
- ❏ goes well with ham and cheese
- ❏ fixes your computer
- ❏ fills you up

Now go back and circle the things on that list that Jesus does (hint: there are two of them).

In John 6:35, Jesus says of himself: "I am the bread of life. He who comes to me will never go hungry, and he who believes in me will never be thirsty." What's it mean for Jesus to be like bread? Catch him in the act of being like bread in these stories—

Read John 19:25-27.

Who was hungry?

What was she hungry for?

How did Jesus satisfy her hunger?

Read Luke 19:2-9.

Who was hungry?

What was he hungry for?

How did Jesus satisfy his hunger?

Read Mark 8:22-25.

Who was hungry?

What was he hungry for?

How did Jesus satisfy his hunger?

53

Hi, i'm Bread

the name of the person who has a hunger	the hunger the person has	my plan for meeting the need

✂ -

WiLDPAGE

Hi, i'm Bread

the name of the person who has a hunger	the hunger the person has	my plan for meeting the need

54

Lesson 8

God is like a TEAM CAPTAIN

But you are a chosen people, a royal priesthood, a holy nation, a people belonging to God, that you may declare the praises of him who called you out of darkness into his wonderful light. —*1 Peter 2:9*

Goals

STUDENTS WILL—

- Understand why God pictures himself as a team captain.
- Think about what it means to include people who aren't normally included.
- Write an action plan for making someone feel included this week.

Picture Prep

Team captain creation

If your group has more than a dozen kids, divide them into teams of about six. If your group has fewer than that, adjust accordingly (if you group has five or fewer kids, just do this exercise as a noncompetitive game with all the kids working together). Give each team a six-foot piece of butcher paper and a set of markers. Give them the following instructions—

- Choose a sport and a name for their team.
- Draw a team captain by having one of their team members lie down on the paper and outlining them, then drawing on a team uniform.
- Label all the things that make this person a great team captain—smart, with an arrow to the head; good listener, with an arrow to an ear, and so on.
- Give the captain a name. Give the teams about five minutes to draw their captains. Then have each team appoint an assistant captain to introduce the captain to everyone else. Have this person explain the good qualities of their captain.

You'll Need—

- Large pieces of butcher paper
- Set of markers for each team of six kids

Wrap up this section by reviewing with these questions—

So, what characteristics does a great team captain have? Those of you who have played on a team of some sort, what difference has it made if you've had a good or a not-so-good team captain?

There's one more segue to make, but with a caution to you. This self-portrait of God centers around the idea that he has picked us to be on his team. You're going to ask a couple questions about picking teams. This is a *big-time* sensitive issue. If you've always been one of those people who were picked early when groups divided into teams, you have no idea how badly the kids who get picked last feel. Kids who get picked last—or even halfway through—have their self-images systematically crushed and stomped and squished and mangled and spit upon.

This lesson is almost more important for them than anyone else, because it's so great for them to know God has chosen them for his team. But you need to be very sensitive when talking about this (especially if you're a super-

athletic type and all your kids know it). Plunge right into how awesome God is for picking any of us. And be extra-sure that there is no gloating by those who might get picked early for sports teams. So...say something like this—

Have you ever been in a situation where teams were being picked? It's a tense situation. Everyone wants to be picked early; no one wants to be picked late. *[If you were a got-picked-late kid, tell your students.]* **It's really a cruel way to divide up teams. But here's the cool news: we're going to see today how God individually picked you to be on his team!**

Action shot

Rebus time

In case this is new turf for you, a rebus is a sentence spelled out in pictures.

Pass out copies of **Rebus Time** (page 59) and pens or pencils to your kids. Let them work in twos or threes to solve the puzzles. There are two Bible verses on the page. To decode them, they need to say the little pictures out loud, subtract and add letters as instructed, and figure out what the real word would be. Let them work at it until at least half of the group has finished; then have someone read them, and have those who weren't finished fill in the remaining blanks.

The first verse is 1 Peter 2:9: "But you are a chosen people,

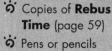

a royal priesthood, a holy nation, a people belonging to God." The second verse is Colossians 3:12: "Therefore, as God's chosen people, holy and dearly loved..." Yup, this could take a little while! Go get yourself some coffee! (Or you can just do one verse or the other if you're pressed for time.)

After everyone has the right verses filled in the blanks, ask—

Why would God pick you and me to be on his team?
God picked us just because he loves us.

What difference does it make to you that God picked you?

What difference does it make that he picked you, but he didn't pick you because of your ability or goodness?
It should give us confidence that his love isn't conditional; it should give us peace. Of course, these answers are probably way too deep for your kids—they'll probably say something like, "Um, it's cool."

Ask your students to turn in their Bibles to Colossians 3:12 and read the whole verse. Ask—

Therefore, as God's chosen people, holy and dearly loved, clothe yourselves with compassion, kindness, humility, gentleness and patience.
Colossians 3:12

A theological thought
In the Old Testament, as you probably know, God worked fairly exclusively with the people of Israel—his chosen people. But with the coming of Jesus, the team roster was lengthened a bit—God decided to include you and me in the designation *chosen people.*

Now, if you ever meet me, you very well might ask, "Why in the world would God choose him?" You'd be right to ask that question, as I might be to ask about you! Because none of us *deserve* to be on God's team. Not only should we be the last ones picked, we shouldn't even make the cut. So, to use ridiculous understatement, it's pretty neat-o that he chose us!

How should we respond to being picked by God?

Thankfulness, of course; but we should be willing to follow his lead.

☼ What does the team captain want of us?

To "clothe ourselves with compassion, kindness, humility, gentleness, and patience."

☼ What does that mean? Why does the Bible say* clothe *yourself with these things?*

It's poetic language for becoming these things, putting them on yourself.

Self-portrait

Remind students that we should be able to see a small portion of God's character in ourselves, since he made us in his image. Then ask—

☼ So what characteristic is the team captain portrait showing? What does this image reveal about God?

This isn't an easy question, and your kids might not have a clue—even though you just talked about it (this situation of not having a clue what they just talked about is a regularly recurring theme in junior high ministry!). The idea isn't that God is good at picking teams. The idea is that God includes people who don't deserve to be included. It's a grace picture, really.

☼ What would this characteristic look like in a teenager?

Again, this is a toughie, and many of your kids won't have any idea how to answer this question

(that's okay). The answer, of course, revolves around showing grace and acceptance to others—including and loving people who haven't done anything to deserve it. But for the purposes of this lesson, we'll focus in on including people.

Picking my team

Pass out copies of **Picking My Team** (page 60) to each student, and make sure they all have something to write with. Ask them to forget about everything you've talked about for the past half hour—for a few minutes. They should read through the list of possible friends and put a star next to the five they would choose. Tell them not to try to be spiritual or give the answers they think you want. They should star the ones they would really choose. By the way, the descriptions are short, and you might think at first that there's not enough to go on for kids to make choices. But they will picture someone at their school who is like these descriptions, and mentally fill in the blanks, creating a picture in their minds of what these kids are like.

You'll Need—

- ☼ Copies of **Picking My Team** (page 60)
- ☼ Pens or pencils

Ideally, you'll be able to utilize small groups to debrief this exercise (with an adult leader in each one). But one of the first rules of junior high ministry is "make do with what you've got!" So if you can't pull together small groups, don't sweat it.

Either way, read the names of the students on **Picking My Team** and have your kids raise their hands to show whether they included that person on their teams.

Now have everyone look over the list a second time and put a cross next to the students they think God would pick to be on his team. Give this instruction without much more explanation—it's a trick question. Your kids will probably assume they're only supposed to pick five again and will look for the biggest losers in the list. This isn't a bad assumption on their part—after all, our God loves the outcast and the downtrodden! But the trick is this—God picks everyone! Not just the losers, not just the winners. He picks *each of us* to be on his team.

So after your kids have selected God's team, debrief this list the same way you did the first one—read the names of the imaginary students and have your kids raise their hands to indicate which ones God would pick. The truth of this exercise may become clear to some of your kids during this hand-raising, as they realize that God wouldn't leave out kids like the hand-raising shows. After you've gone through the list, ask—

☼ **Are there any students on this list God wouldn't pick to be on his team?**
Nope. Have your kids go back over the list and add crosses next to all the names.

Now choose a couple imaginary students, and brainstorm with your group how they could reach out and include each of them. Ask your students for suggestions on how they could connect with each kid—how they could make the kid feel like he or she were picked instead of picked on!

Picking, for real

Move to personal application by having students think of someone in their school who doesn't get picked very often—not for teams, not for friendship, not for conversation. Have them write that name down on the top of their paper. They should write down three different ideas for how they could make that person feel included and chosen.

The ideas have to be doable and specific. In other words, they can't write, "Have everyone in the school be nice to him" (not doable) or "I'll be nice to her" (not specific enough). After they've thought of three possibilities, ask them to circle one they'll commit to trying this week. Tell them to add when and where to the idea they circled. Debrief in small groups if possible. Be careful, as the kids they want to reach out to could be in your group! The last thing you want is for some kid to say, "I'm going to reach out to Jimmy, 'cause he's such a loser—just look at him over there!"

As always, make sure you close your time in prayer, thanking God for picking us to be on his team and asking for courage to follow through with our action plans.

You'll Need—

☼ The back of **Picking My Team** from the last activity, or blank paper
☼ Pens or pencils

Room decoration option
If you're using the graphic option described in Lesson 1, add a large graphic of a team (a group of people in uniform) with *Captain* written clearly across the uniform of someone in the middle.

Rebus Time

Sound out the pictures below and try to write the words of these two verses into the blanks.

 – terfly   U   R   A   ch +  – r + n    ,

_____

a +  ,   a + y  + tion

_____

a 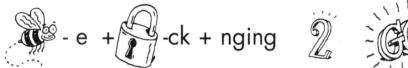 – e + -ck + nging   2

_____ ☺ ☺ ☺ ☺ _____

There +    as  +'s   ch + – r + n    ,

___ ___ ___ ___ ___ ___ ___ ___ ___ ___

 – e + y   &    + ly    + d...

_____

(59)

Picking My Team

Charise is bubbly and talkative. She's cute and outgoing and has lots of friends. Charise isn't mean to people but mainly hangs out with popular kids.

Brennan is developmentally challenged. He's in eighth grade but acts and thinks and talks like a third grader. He's nice to absolutely everybody.

Jeff likes drama. He's a nice guy, but he's not popular at all. He's pretty serious about his relationship with God and is active in his youth group at church.

Tina is, like, the shortest and smallest girl in the whole school. Kids laugh about her all the time. But she's a really nice girl and outgoing.

Paco is a skateboarding maniac. He's totally into hardcore music and radical stuff. He's usually got scrapes and bruises from trying impossible skateboard tricks.

Lauren is into black stuff. She wears only black clothes, lots of dark makeup, and listens to dark music. She never smiles and looks mad most of the time.

Chrissy is a soccer freak. She lives and breathes soccer—and is great at it. She's really athletic and doesn't care about her looks or what people think about her looks.

James is serious and quiet. He's one of the smartest kids in the whole school. His only friends are other serious, quiet, and smart kids.

Grace is second-generation Chinese-American (her parents came from China and do not speak English). She struggles with living in two worlds—her Chinese home and her American school.

Tim is average—in every way. Not loud, not quiet. He's got a few friends but not that many. He's an average student. He's not on any sports teams or in any clubs, and no one usually notices him.

Tran is a fantastic guitar player. He's got a band, and they're really good. He looks very cool—like a rock star. But he's super-quiet and hardly ever talks.

Ruby just won't shut up. She is constantly talking. She's a nice girl but is known to gossip a lot too. The girls she hangs around with all talk a lot, too.

Greg doesn't seem to have any friends. He sits by himself at lunch and never seems to talk to anyone. If he disappeared from school, no one would notice.

Jill is way overweight. She's pretty shy, too. Kids make fun of her all the time, and she really doesn't seem to have any friends.

60

God is like a BEST FRIEND

Greater love has no one than this, that he lay down his life for his friends. —*John 15:13*

Goals

STUDENTS WILL—

- Understand that because God treats us as best friends, he shares everything with us.
- Decide which qualities make up a best friend.
- Choose a way they can improve their friend-character this week.

Picture Prep

Famous friends

Distribute copies of **Famous Friends** (page 65), and pens or pencils (or crayons or eyeliner pencils or ink-producing squid and quill-like feathers) to each student. Allow them to work in pairs to match as many of the friends as they can.

As a variation, this would be a great game to convert to PowerPoint slides and play as teams.

Here are the answers—

You'll Need—

- Copies of **Famous Friends** (page 65)
- Pens or pencils

Famous Friends

Match up these famous friends. They can be from real life, the Bible, movies, TV, cartoons, books, or other sources.

Bert and *Ernie*		Balloo
Paul and *Barnabas*		Barnabas
Laurel and *Hardy*		Barney Rubble
Mowgli and *Balloo*		Bullwinkle
Siskel and *Ebert*		Clark
Batman and *Robin*		Dean Martin
Jerry Lewis and *Dean Martin*		Ebert
Fred Flintstone and *Barney Rubble*		Ernie
C3PO and *R2D2*		Ethel Mertz
Hansel and *Gretel*		Gretel
Scooby Doo and *Shaggy*		Hardy
Henry Kissinger and *Richard Nixon*		Jack Lemmon
LaVerne and *Shirley*		Jonathan
Garfield and *Odie*		Mickey
David and *Jonathan*		Odie
Rocky and *Bullwinkle*		Pokey
Snoopy and *Woodstock*		R2D2
Lucy Ricardo and *Ethel Mertz*		Richard Nixon
Gumby and *Pokey*		Robin
Walter Matthau and *Jack Lemmon*		Shaggy
Pluto and *Mickey*		Shirley
Lewis and *Clark*		Woodstock

(65)

Action shot

Active option
Balloon stomp

This is a classic youth group game—tie a balloon around the ankle of your students and have them protect their own while trying to stomp and break others. But in this *friendship* twist on the game, have students get in pairs (be sensitive to kids without friends in your group). Their challenge is to make sure their partner's balloon doesn't break. Give the extra balloons or string to the team that wins.

Make a transition by saying something like—

Obviously, we're talking about friends today. But specifically, we're talking about how God is like a best friend to us.

You'll Need—

ම One balloon for each kid

ම Some string

Ask—

ම **What's the difference between a friend and a best friend?**
A best friend is someone who you can really count on, someone who knows all about you and still likes you.

ම **How is God like a best friend?**

ම **How can you have a best friend who you can't even see?**
This is a very difficult question, without a great obvious answer. It's asked here more to give verbalization to a question some of the kids will already have in their minds.

Verse rewrite

Pass out copies of **What's the Difference?** (page 66) and writing tools (a.k.a. small weapons of mass destruction) to your students. Allow them to work in pairs or trios to complete the paraphrasing described on the sheet.

Here's the skinny—in this verse, God (Jesus) describes himself as a best friend because he shares everything with us. This is different than what you would do with an acquaintance or an enemy or a servant.

By rewriting this verse, hopefully (yeah, it's always hopeful that your kids will get the point!) your students will gain an understanding of both the basis of real friendship and the basis of their potential friendship with God.

You'll Need—

ම Copies of **What's the Difference?** (page 66)

ම Pens or pencils

Option
Modify this exercise by assigning one relationships to each small group of kids and asking them to rewrite the verse. For instance, you would tell the first small group to rewrite the verse as if we were only acquaintances with Jesus. The second group rewrites the verse as if we were robots. You get the idea, right?

Have groups share their paraphrases with the whole group. Then ask these questions—

ම **So what difference does it make that God wants to be our best friend?**

ම **How many people does it take to have best friends?**
This is a silly question, really. Obviously, it takes at least two people. But the point is—you can't have best friends if only one of the people wants it. God is pursuing us and wants to be best friends with us.

But the friendship only becomes real if we pursue it also!

🔆 **God's done a lot to prove to us that he wants to be our best friend. What can we do to show him we want the same thing?**

🔆 **How important is trustworthiness? Similarity?**
And so on.

🔆 **Which are the top three, in your opinion? Which aren't important at all?**

Paperless option
Yup, you can do this without paper if you want. You'll need the 10 characteristics written somewhere kids can see them (on an overhead, PowerPoint slide, tattooed on your back). Either have kids respond verbally or create a room-sized scale and have them move to indicate their response.

Self-portrait

Best friend characteristics

Remind your students of the assumptions behind this series of lessons—God has given us self-portraits of himself in Scripture (we just looked at one) that help us get to know him and his character better. Because we're created in the image of God, we should be able to find these characteristics in ourselves also—just like we can see characteristics of our earthly parents in ourselves. This self-portrait— as best friend—is a little more obvious. We can all picture ourselves as best friends (whether we are one or not). But we often don't think about the fact that being a good friend, or a best friend, is a reflection of God. We are like God when we are best friends. And God wants us to have best friendships.

Give 'em copies of **Best Friend Stuff** (page 67) and something to write with. The explanation on the sheet is pretty clear—they should rate each of the possible characteristics of a best friend on a 1-10 scale, adding an additional characteristic if they want to. Then they should go back and rank the top three and cross out any unimportant ones. After kids have had a few minutes to complete this, debrief it by asking questions like—

Print it!

Me, best friend?

Once again (I know I'm harping on this), be cautious of kids who don't have many or any friends. You might want to say something like—

Not everyone has tons of friends. Certainly not everyone has best friends at all times. Our point today isn't that something is wrong with you if you don't have best friends! Instead, we want to develop this God-like characteristic of *being* a best friend–even if we don't have one right now.

»

It's extra-important that you're sensitive to kids in your group who don't have many, if any, friends. Loners are more and more common these days. And to speak of best friends as a norm can be really hurtful to them. They already feel like freaks most of the time—and the last thing we want to do is communicate that God, the church, and their youth leaders think the same of them. So think through your language on this one. Talk in terms of "developing the characteristic of being a best friend."

You'll Need—

🔆 Copies of **Best Friend Stuff** (page 67)

🔆 You guessed it (you're sooo smart!)—pens or pencils

You'll Need—

- Copies of **Best Friend Stuff** (page 67), from the last activity
- Pens or pencils

Have your students look over the list of characteristics on **Best Friend Stuff** again. Have them customize the list in two more ways.

First, have them underline the characteristics they're pretty good at. These would be words friends might use to describe them. This, of course, is a great small-group discussion (hint, hint). Then after you've debriefed a bit, have them look over the list again and circle any characteristics they need to work on—one or two (or more) they could show some improvement in.

Second, have them choose one characteristic they're going to do something about this week. Ask students to turn their papers over and write that characteristic at the top of the blank page. Then ask them to write the name of someone and a plan for putting this characteristic into action this week. Push them to make their plan concrete and doable. If your group has 10 or fewer kids, ask if a few will share their plans. If your group is larger than 10, consider sharing these in smaller groups. It would be great if you could revisit this next week to see how it went.

Check for understanding by asking these questions—

Why does God care about this?

It's quite simple, really. These are characteristics of God; and he wants us to be like him. And, because he loves us so much, he wants us to experience the joy of great friendships. It's one of his gifts to us!

How can best friendships be bad?

When they exclude others and are mean to other people.

Close your time in prayer thanking God for his friendship. (It's an amazing thing, isn't it?) If you have time, you might want to ask kids to write out prayers of thanks to God for his friendship and ask him to help them with their friendship action plans.

Room decoration option

If you're using the graphic option described in Lesson 1, add a large picture of Bert and Ernie or any other pair from **Famous Friends** (page 65) or even a generic twosome connected together.

Famous Friends

Match up these famous friends. They can be from real life, the Bible, movies, TV,
cartoons, books, or other sources.

Bert and _____	Balloo
Paul and _____	Barnabas
Laurel and _____	Barney Rubble
Mowgli and _____	Bullwinkle
Siskel and _____	Clark
Batman and _____	Dean Martin
Jerry Lewis and _____	Ebert
Fred Flintstone and _____	Ernie
C3PO and _____	Ethel Mertz
Hansel and _____	Gretel
Scooby Doo and _____	Hardy
Henry Kissinger and _____	Jack Lemmon
LaVerne and _____	Jonathan
Garfield and _____	Mickey
David and _____	Odie
Rocky and _____	Pokey
Snoopy and _____	R2D2
Lucy Ricardo and _____	Richard Nixon
Gumby and _____	Robin
Walter Matthau and _____	Shaggy
Pluto and _____	Shirley
Lewis and _____	Woodstock

What's the Difference?

In John 15:15, Jesus says, "I no longer call you servants, because a servant does not know his master's business. Instead, I have called you friends, for everything that I learned from my Father I have made known to you."

He says this to prove we're best friends with him. How might this verse be written if we weren't best friends with him but instead were—

Just acquaintances

Enemies

Robots

Friends, but not best friends

66

Best Friend Stuff

1. Rate these characteristics to show how important they are to being a best friend (1 means not important even the tiniest bit; 10 means 110% mega-important).

____ **Trustworthiness** *you can count on your friend*

____ **Confidentiality** *keeps secrets*

____ **Similarity** *likes the same things you do and is like you in other ways too*

____ **Humor** *fun to be with*

____ **Open** *shares life and thoughts and deep stuff*

____ **Nonjudgmental** *accepts you as you are*

____ **Builder** *helps you be a better person*

____ **Availability** *has time for a close friendship*

____ **Proximity** *yeah, it's a big word; it means "nearby"*

____ **Listener** *this one's obvious, right?*

2. Rank the top three most important characteristics by writing them here.

  1._____

  2._____

  3._____

3. Cross out the characteristics you don't think are important in a best friend (if any).

God is like a GUIDE

I will lead the blind by ways they have not known, along unfamiliar paths I will guide them; I will turn the darkness into light before them and make the rough places smooth. —*Isaiah 42:16*

STUDENTS WILL—

Goals

- Discover that it's hard to hear God's voice in the midst of our noisy and busy lives.
- Learn that God can be trusted to lead them the right way every time.
- Practice giving others sound advice.

Picture Prep

Noisy trust walk

For this exercise, you can use as many teams of four to seven players as you'd like: just one, as an example for everyone to see, or if you have time, teams to accommodate all the kids in your group so they can all experience this exercise firsthand. Write one of the following phrases on each slip of paper or index card.

- SHOUT OUT ALL OF YOUR INSTRUCTIONS, BUT DON'T BOTHER TELLING THE RUNNER ABOUT *EVERY* OBSTACLE ON THE COURSE.
- SHOUT INSTRUCTIONS WHENEVER YOUR RUNNER IS ABOUT TO RUN INTO SOMETHING.
- USE YOUR NORMAL TONE OF VOICE, BUT SEE HOW MANY THINGS YOU CAN GET THE RUNNER TO BUMP INTO!
- USE A NORMAL TONE OF VOICE AND TRY TO GET YOUR RUNNER TO THE FINISH LINE THE FASTEST!
- SHH! WHISPER DIRECTIONS IN THE RUNNER'S EAR AND DO YOUR BEST TO KEEP THE RUNNER FROM GETTING HURT ON THE COURSE.
- WHISPER INTO THE RUNNER'S EAR, BUT TELL HER THE WRONG WAY TO GO.

You'll Need—

- Blindfolds
- Slips of paper or index cards
- A variety of obstacles such as chairs, tables, trash cans, blankets

Set up an obstacle course that runs the length of your room—with lots of things for students to climb over and under, run around, and so on. Your kids should know just by looking at the course that this won't be a piece of cake!

One kid from each team should be chosen to travel the course and then blindfolded. The others will walk alongside the blindfolded player, offering instructions and directions. However, as you can see from the phrases that are written on the instruction cards, some helpers will be of more assistance than others.

Just before each team runs the course, blindfold the runner and let the nonrunners choose a card. They should read the instructions to themselves, then return the card to you for the next team to use. The helpers shouldn't tell anyone what their card says.

Now let the chaos begin!

When your time is up, bring the students back together to debrief. Ask the runners—

What was it like to wear the blindfold during the race?

- ☼ How long did it take you to figure out who was guiding you through the course correctly?

- ☼ Were you able to hear that person's voice over the others?

- ☼ Did you ever stop listening to everyone and just try to do it on your own?

- ☼ How did that work?

Ask the helpers—

- ☼ How did it feel to compete with all the others who were guiding your runner?

- ☼ Were you frustrated when the runner didn't do what you said?

- ☼ How did it feel to lead them astray?

Action shot

Old Testament navigation

A^{sk—}

You'll Need—

- ☼ Bibles
- ☼ Paper (half-sheets are enough)
- ☼ Pens or pencils

Have you ever been lost? What happened? How did you feel? How did you find your way? *Kids will love telling their stories, so be prepared to let only a few volunteers share.*

Next, talk a little bit about how travelers from long

ago would use the stars in the sky to guide them—for example, sailors used the constellations like maps of the sky. And don't forget the three kings who used just a single bright star to guide them as they traveled from far away to find Jesus.

Now make a transition by telling the kids that when we need guidance—not so much the physical kind, but in making good decisions during our lives—we can look to God and ask him to show us the way.

Divide the kids into small groups of students (ideally with an adult leader in each one—just to keep things on track!). Assign each group one of the following six Scripture passages that talk about trusting God for guidance. If your group is small and you only assign, say, three of these—don't sweat it!

Psalm 25:1-6	**Psalm 48:9-14**
Psalm 73:21-26	**Psalm 139:1-10**
Proverbs 4:10-13	**Isaiah 58:9-11**

Each group should read their passage aloud and discuss what it says about God's guidance. Then have the groups summarize their verses and the contents to the whole group.

By now your students should understand that it can be tough to give good advice to people, but it's not tough for God. He knows everything! And the best part is that he loves each of us so much that he's not going to steer us the wrong way when we ask him to guide us.

Now pass out blank paper (half sheets are enough) and pens or pencils to your students. Have each kid choose one of the six verses just used. You might want to write them on a whiteboard (or a PowerPoint slide if you live in the new millennium!). To help your kids remember that God is the perfect, all-knowing, and loving guide for their lives, have them rewrite their chosen verse in their own words, making it a modern-day psalm that will remind them to seek God's help the next time they feel lost.

When they've finished, ask for a few student volunteers to read theirs to the group. Remind the kids that they'll meet people throughout their day who need guidance—and, more importantly, they need God! Encourage them to ask God to guide and give them wisdom whenever they're asked to give advice or share their opinion about something.

Self-portrait

Guide group, international

Pass out copies of **Guide Group, International** (page 73) and pens or pencils to your students. (As the case in previous lessons, this exercise could be done verbally if you don't want to give handouts to your kids.) Explain that this is a made-up group of teens who've put together an advice-giving company. As a group, read the first scenario and have your kids rate the advice given. Then have your kids act as consultants to GGI by giving them input on the second scenario. Have several kids read their advice to GGI.

You'll Need—

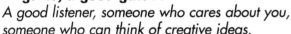

ö Copies of **Guide Group, International** (page 73)

ö Pens or pencils

Now have a discussion about how to give good advice. Ask—

ö What characteristics make a good advice-giver, a good guide?
A good listener, someone who cares about you, someone who can think of creative ideas.

ö How do you know if someone needs guidance?
Of course, they might ask—that's easiest—or it might be obvious that someone doesn't know what to do.

ö What do you do if someone obviously needs some advice but hasn't asked for it?
You ask if he or she would like your input.

ö What are some of the most important things you can tell someone?
Pray; get the advice of wise people (parents, teachers, pastors); see what the Bible says.

Say something like—

Remember, being a guide often doesn't mean that you tell people the decision they should make. More than that, it means you help point people in the right direction to find the answer they need. And you can especially help them by pointing them to God!

Print it!

Dear teen adviser

Now it's your students' turn to give some good advice. Hand out copies of **Dear Teen Adviser** (pages 74-75) and something to write with to each student. This worksheet will transform your students into nationally syndicated advice columnists for teens (woo-hoo!). There are four letters for them to read and respond to with a brief letter of advice.

Have the kids work on their sheets by themselves for about eight or 10 minutes and then let them share some of their answers within their small groups. Ask—

ö How does it make you feel when others ask you for advice?
Flattered, stressed out, important, nervous, needed.

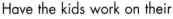

You'll Need—

ö Copies of **Dear Teen Adviser** (pages 74-75)

ö Pens or pencils

☺ When you're asked to help someone figure something out, do you ever suggest they ask God for help?

☺ Do you pray about it and ask God to help you before you respond to a request for help? How can you remember to do that?

Close the discussion with prayer. Pray that your students will seek God's guidance before they try to guide others and that he'll give them the wisdom and other godly traits they need to be good advisers.

It might be a good idea to take a moment to discuss some of the tougher issues that may come up with your teens and what their options are before they're asked to respond in some way.

What should they do if a friend tells them about wanting to commit suicide? What is the best response if they catch a girlfriend making herself throw up after a meal? How can they react in a godly way when their buddy can't get through a day of school without a drink?

These are times when it's best to bring a trusted adult into the equation. They shouldn't be afraid to seek help on someone's behalf—it could be a matter of life and death.

Room decoration option

Make a large star covered with aluminum foil to represent the ones that travelers used to guide them on their journeys. In the same way the Magi looked at the star for guidance when they were searching for the baby in the manger, your students can to look to the star-maker—God—for guidance.

Guide Group, International

Hi! We're a group of five teenagers who started Guide Group, International (GGI) to give advice to people. Here's one of our recent clients and the advice we gave her. We value your input. Would you please rate our advice?

Dear Guide Group, International,

I'm trying to figure out what I should do about this guy I like. He doesn't go to church, and I'm pretty sure he's not a Christian. My parents have always told me they want me to be careful about dating non-Christians. My youth worker said something like this recently too, but I don't remember why, really. But the guy's really cute! What should I do?

Sincerely,

Hannah

Dear Hannah,

Well, it sounds like you need to do some investigation work! We'd advise you to go to three sources—the Bible, your parents, and your youth leader. Go to your parents, and ask them to explain their feelings about this again—it's important for you to understand where they're coming from. Then go to your youth worker and ask him or her to explain it again too. Then ask your youth worker to show you how to find what the Bible might say about this—and look at it for yourself. You might read a book on the subject too—there are some great ones written for Christian teens like yourself (a Christian bookstore could help you find one). Don't forget to pray about it, Hannah!

What do you think of our guidance?

LOUSY ADVICE!   NOT TOO BAD   OKAY ADVICE   GREAT ADVICE!

Now, here's a current client seeking guidance.

Dear GGI,

I really need your advice! I'm thinking about getting a job. It's just a little thing—the florist down the street from my house needs someone to clean up the back room in the store every afternoon for about an hour. The money would be really cool to have. My parents said it's up to me, but they're worried that I'm a little young to have a job every day of the week. It might cut into my ability to be involved in anything at school, too.

What would you tell Colton?

Dear Colton,

Dear Teen Adviser

You are a nationally syndicated advice columnist for teens. Below are four of the letters that just arrived in the mail. Read them over and then write a brief letter of advice to each one for this week's column.

Dear Teen Adviser,

I don't know what to do! My mom and dad have been divorced for almost a year now, and it wasn't a very friendly breakup. They're always telling my sister and me about how awful the other one is and how we shouldn't believe anything they say. Whenever they're in the same room with each other, they glare and say mean things. Usually they end up shouting at each other until one of them stomps away and slams the door.

Well, I just found out that I've won a writing award, and there is going to be a big ceremony at my school in a couple weeks. We're only allowed to invite two guests, but I'm not sure I want my mom and dad sitting together and ruining my big night. What should I do?

Sincerely,

Torn between Two Parents in Denver

Dear Torn,

Dear Teen Adviser,

I'm the youngest in my family. My dad is a lawyer, my mom is a stockbroker, and all my older brothers and sisters are straight-A students. I get pretty good grades too, but not like the rest of my family. I mean, I try hard in school, but it doesn't come easily for me. What I really like to do is work on the yearbook, play volleyball, and rehearse my lines for the upcoming musical. These are the things that really get me going!

My parents just don't understand, though. Last night they grounded me for three weeks because I got a C+ on my science project. Now I can't talk to my friends on the phone, and they told me I have to drop two of my after-school commitments because they're taking up time I should be spending studying! It's so unfair! How can I make them understand that I may not be like everyone else in my family, but that I'm still okay?

Sincerely,

Grounded and Misunderstood in Maine

Dear Grounded,

74

(page 1)

Dear Teen Adviser,

I just moved to this town a month ago. I still don't know too many people in my school. Moving is bad enough, but to change schools in the middle of the year has been really tough. Everyone is already grouped off with friends they've known forever, and it doesn't seem like anyone's looking to add a new kid to their group.

But "Ray" has been kind of nice to me. He's in my art class and says he really likes my drawings. He said he'll help me when we start doing watercolors next month because he's really good at it. Two days ago Ray invited me to hang out with him and his friends in the park on Saturday. At first I was really excited. Nobody's invited me to do anything for weeks.

But then I overheard some guys in the locker room talking about how Ray is the guy to ask when you need some good drugs or beer for a party. Now I don't know what to do. Ray's been really cool in class, but I don't drink, and I've never tried drugs before. What do I do?

Sincerely,

Alone and Confused in Kalamazoo

Dear Alone,

Dear Teen Adviser,

I've been a buddy with "Trevor" since kindergarten. We do everything together! We're always hanging out at each other's houses, we play the same sports, and we have almost every class together. Right after school started, Trevor noticed this cool girl in his math class, "Sherry." She had just transferred here from another state. He started calling her on the weekends, and then he invited her to hang out with us sometimes—not a lot, but once in a while.

I like Sherry okay, but lately I've noticed her flirting with me when Trevor isn't around. She laughs a lot at the stuff I say, she touches my arm way more than she needs to, and she's always flipping her hair over her shoulder. Last night Sherry called me. She said she's liked me since the first day we met, and then she invited me to the school dance! I totally know that Trevor plans to ask her to that dance! How do I get out of this mess?

Sincerely,

Afraid to Lose a Friend in Jacksonville

Dear Afraid,

God is like a KiNG

I am the Lord, your Holy One, Israel's Creator, your King.
—Isaiah 43:15

Goals

STUDENTS WiLL—
- Take a closer look at the good and bad qualities of human kings in the Old Testament and how they compare to God—the perfect king.
- Think about what qualities a king should have.
- Find some ways to exhibit kingly qualities in their daily lives.

Picture Prep

Whatta king!

Test your students' kingly trivia knowledge with a rousing game of Whatta King! (Can you feel the excitement? It's pulsating, isn't it?) This game is made up of rounds of play, and each round contains two questions—a youth group or church trivia question tailored to your kids and a Whatta King! question (see sample questions at right) about various kings in the Bible. Oh yeah, and this game is played with two teams—one side of the room against the other.

First, you'll need to come up with some trivia questions that most of your students should know the answers to. Make them sequentially more difficult. Start with super easy ones like, "How many kids does the youth pastor have?" Move, in subsequent rounds through medium difficulty questions, like "What was the theme of last year's summer camp?" In the final rounds, have difficult

but still knowable questions, like "What's the name of the senior pastor's dog?" You get the idea.

Now come up with some tougher questions about some biblical kings—good and bad kings (or use the questions in this sidebar). Use more obscure questions in later rounds because they'll be worth more points.

Sample Whatta King! Questions

Round 1
For one point—This king killed a giant with only a slingshot and a stone. (David)

Round 2
For two points—Who was King David's best friend? (Jonathan)

Round 3
For three points—This king wrote a large portion of the Book of Proverbs in the Bible. (King Solomon)

Round 4
For four points—This man was the first to be appointed king of Israel. (King Saul)

Round 5
For five points—Who replaced King Saul? (King David)

Round 6
For six points—This famous king of Babylon ordered three young Israelite men to walk into a fiery furnace. (King Nebuchadnezzar)

For 10 bonus points—spell King Nebuchadnezzar's name.

You'll Need—
- A list of trivia questions
- A list of **Whatta King** questions
- A pack of king-sized (get it?) candy bars for a prize

However, you may wish to make those multiple-choice questions, just so it isn't impossible for your kids to answer. You know how much or how little your kids know about the Bible, so just plan accordingly.

The number of trivia and Whatta King! questions will be determined by how many rounds you wish to play. Make sure you have one of each kind of question for every round. No points are given for correctly answering the trivia questions, but whichever contestant is the first to stand up and correctly answer a youth group trivia question is given the chance to answer a Whatta King! question for team points.

For a twist on the rules, you can include the challenge option. After a Bible-related question is read—but before it's answered—the opposing team can wager some or all of their points on whether the contestant will answer correctly. If they guess correctly, they add as many points as they wagered to their score. If they guess incorrectly, they have to subtract that many points.

When the game is over, award king-size candy bars to the winning team. Make sure the kids get the connection.

Then make a transition. It's difficult for kids to imagine living under the rule of a king who has complete authority over them. Stink! We can't imagine it either! So to get them thinking, ask a few volunteers to share their responses to the following questions—

ö **What's your definition of a king?**

ö **Does anyone know the difference between a constitutional monarchy and an absolute monarchy?**
In an absolute monarchy, the king can do anything. What he says is the law. A constitutional monarch is more of a figurehead, like the Queen of England.

ö **How is a king different than a president [or prime minister if you live in a country that has that position]?**

ö **Who are the people in your life who can tell you what to do?**
Parents, teachers, coaches, bosses, policemen, city mayor, state senator, the president.

ö **How do you feel when you're being told what to do by these people?**

ö **What do you think it means that God is like a king?**

We three kings

Before your students can think about God as a king, it might be helpful for them to look at the lives of some human kings first. Since our country hasn't been under the rule of a monarchy for over 200 years, direct them to the Old Testament and the stories of three kings of biblical proportions.

First give them a little background information about how the nation of Israel looked around and decided they didn't want to stand out from other nations any longer. They wanted to have a flesh-and-blood ruler to follow instead of allowing their almighty and perfect Creator to continue leading them (*what were they thinking?*).

Divide your group into small groups of five or more (it would be good if you had at least 3 groups, so adjust the size accordingly). Ideally, you'll have an adult in each group also (unless your junior highers are from a different universe than most!). Give each group a copy of **Good King, Bad King** (page 81) and something to write with.

You'll Need—

ö Copies of the **Good King, Bad King** (page 81)
ö Pens or pencils
ö Whiteboard and markers (optional)

Using the Old Testament, students should skim the applicable Old Testament book for information about one of the following kings of Israel: Saul (1 Samuel), David (2 Samuel), or Solomon (1 Kings). Give them 10 to 15 minutes to try to answer as many questions as they can. They should feel free to add any other interesting information they find during their search.

After their time is up, ask a few groups to share their findings with everyone. Ask them how they would feel if they were living as an Israelite under each king's rule. Would they be scared? Would they trust their king? Ask a few students to share how these human kings compare to God as King.

Working in their same small groups, have them use the back of **Good King, Bad King** for this next part. Explain to the students that each group is now a disgruntled group of citizens from an island nation that's ruled by a very evil and nasty king. Before they stage a coup and overthrow this ruler, they need to figure out what kind of ruler they want to put in her place. Ask them to work together to come up with a detailed description of their new ruler.

After they've finished working, hold a summit meeting where all the groups are given a chance to present their ideas for a new ruler to the rest of the island's residents (the other small groups). List some of the characteristics on a whiteboard, if possible. Then spend some time as a whole group comparing the perfect rulers with God the King.

Self-portrait

What would the king do?

Ask students—

☼ Do you ever feel like a king? When?
After a really good day at school; after helping someone; after beating up my little brother.

☼ Why is it hard to imagine feeling like a king?
I don't live in a castle; I don't own a room full of gold and jewels; I'm not the boss of anybody; I'm too young; my parents and teachers tell me what to do.

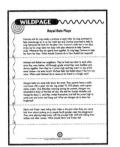

Have students review what they wrote down about the three human kings from the Old Testament, as well as the traits they listed about God as a king on their **Good King, Bad King** (page 81) handout.

Then say something like—

God definitely has kingly qualities, like the ones you listed on your sheets (for instance, he's loyal, strong, powerful, unchanging, loving, trustworthy, hates wickedness, disciplines, is admired or looked up to, keeps his promises regardless of what we do, in control). Since you're made in the image of God, you also have the makings of a king! Think that's impossible? Let's take a look at the royal characteristics of some everyday teens.

Create smaller groups and assign each group a scenario from **Royal Role Plays** (page 82) to create and act out for the rest of the youth group—twice. One version should show a teen behaving in a kingly way—like God the king—and the second should demonstrate some not-so-kingly behavior.

Feel free to come up with role plays of your own as well.

To save time (and if you have a lot of small groups), you could give two groups the same role-play situation and let one act out the kingly behavior, and the other group the opposite. Debrief

☼ Copies of **Good King, Bad King** (page 81), from the last activity
☼ A copy of **Royal Role Plays** (page 82), cut apart
☼ Role-play ideas (see samples, and make up your own)

You'll Need—

each kingly role-play by having the audience name the king-like attributes shown in the drama.

Here's what you might see the kids act out in each scenario.

Cammie's kingly traits of God—God keeps his promises no matter what we do in return; he's trustworthy.

Michael's kingly traits of God—God is loyal and loving toward his people in all circumstances.

Morgan's kingly traits of God—God is trustworthy, hates wickedness, is looked up to and admired.

Devin and Tristan's kingly traits of God—God disciplines those who are wrong; God is strong and powerful; God is looked up to and admired; God hates wickedness.

Royal declaration

Explain to your students that being *kingly* could be misunderstood as being bossy or pushing around others who are weaker than we are. Obviously, that's not good-king behavior (and God is certainly a good king!). Instead, this characteristic should be seen as taking the high road in tough situations, being above using petty and mean behavior to get our own way, and trying to do the right thing (what God wants us to do) no matter who disagrees with you. In other words, it's not easy being king!

Take your students to the next level and focus their attention toward their own king-like behavior. Hand out copies of **Royal Declaration** (page 83) and pencils or pens to each student. This worksheet will ask the kids to examine their relationships and think about the people in their lives who need to get the royal treatment from them, instead of the royal pain in the patootie treatment! The Wildpage will also help them think of ways to act more kingly toward these people.

You'll Need—

○ Copies of **Royal Declaration** (page 83)

○ Pens or pencils

Have the kids spread out and work on these sheets individually for about five minutes. When they've finished, bring them back together and ask a few volunteers to share some of their responses and their royal decrees with the group. Encourage them to place this sheet on their dresser mirror, inside their Bible, or somewhere else where they'll see it regularly and be reminded to be kingly—like God—in how they treat others every day.

End with a time of prayer, asking God to help the kids be kings in their schools, at home, at practice, and wherever else they might spend time. Every time they give others the royal treatment, they're being a light to the world.

Room decoration option

Make a big ol' glittery crown for your wall.

Good King, Bad King

Your leader will assign a king of Israel for you to research. Circle yours.

King Saul **1 Samuel**

King David **2 Samuel**

King Solomon **1 Kings**

Skim the corresponding book of the Old Testament to answer the following questions as completely as you can. Feel free to add other interesting notes of information about the king that aren't covered by the questions below.

A study of _____

1. How did he become king?

2. How old was he at the time?

3. In what ways was he a good king?

4. List any godly traits he had.

5. In what ways was he a bad king?

6. What were some of his great victories and triumphs?

7. What made him bad? What went wrong during his rule?

8. What were some of his failures?

9. What resulted from his mistakes? Who else was affected by his sins?

10. How did God deal with him in the end or what became of him?

11. Now look at one or more of the following psalms and list below some of the traits that are mentioned about God as a king.

Psalm 44   Psalm 45   Psalm 46   Psalm 47

Psalm 48   Psalm 66   Psalm 84   Psalm 93

Royal Role Plays

Cammie and Su Ling made a promise to each other. Su Ling promised to help Cammie get an A on her math test and Cammie promised to help Su Ling memorize her lines for the play. Now Cammie's math test is two days away, but Su Ling's been too busy with play rehearsal to help Cammie study. Whenever they do spend time together, Su Ling begs Cammie to help her learn her lines. What should Cammie do or how should she respond?

- -

Michael and Rafael are neighbors. They've lived next door to each other since they were babies. All through grade school they were buddies and always together. Now they're in junior high and they aren't in any of the same classes—not even lunch! Michael feels like Rafael doesn't like him any more. What could Michael do to reassure his friend in a kingly way?

- -

Morgan baby-sits some kids down the street. Their parents have a really nice house with a pool, hot tub, big screen TV, DVD player, and a great stereo system. One Saturday morning during the summer, Morgan was scheduled to baby-sit the kids all day. She told her friends Michelle and Margarite about it, and they invited themselves and half the junior high to come over and swim and hang out! What can Morgan do to show her kingliness?

- -

Devin and Tristan were riding their bikes in the park when they saw some kids from school picking on a couple fourth graders near the playground. They were playing keep-away with the younger kids' stuff and calling them babies and other names. What should Devin and Tristan do?

Royal Declaration

1. Place a mark in the box next to the people you feel you should give the *royal treatment* by being kingly in their lives (impartial, consistent, trustworthy—remember all those characteristics you discussed earlier?).

Who?   **How?**

❏ My parents
❏ My younger siblings
❏ My older siblings
❏ My cousins
❏ My grandparents
❏ My teachers
❏ My coaches
❏ My principal
❏ Grade school kids
❏ High schoolers
❏ Babies
❏ People in the nursing home
❏ My youth pastor
❏ My small group leader
❏ My friends
❏ Other: _____

2. Choose three of the people or groups of people you marked above who you feel it would be easy for you to give the royal treatment. Under the *How* column, write out a way you can be kingly to them this week.

Now fill this in—

I, King _____, promise to do a better job in my kingly duties.
            (insert your name here)

I plan to give _____ the royal treatment this week by using some of my God-
                        (insert a name here)
given kingly traits to do one or more of the following—

Signed _____   Date _____

(83)

God is like a HUMAN

The Word became flesh and made his dwelling among us.
—John 1:14

STUDENTS WILL—

Goals

- Understand why it makes a difference that God became human.
- Think about the principle behind God becoming human, and think about what it would look like for young teens to *become* something for someone else.
- Make a *becoming* plan to show love to someone.

Picture Prep

Human info

Before your group meets, place a YUP sign on one wall in your room, and a NOPE sign on the opposite wall.

When you're ready to begin, have everyone stand up. Then read the statements from Believe It or Not below, one at a time. After each statement, students should move to the YUP sign or the NOPE sign to express whether they think the statement is true or false.

Believe It or Not

- **A person cannot taste food unless it's mixed with saliva.** *yup*
- **Your stomach has to produce a new layer of mucus every two weeks otherwise it will digest itself.** *yup*
    - **Your hair grows at an average rate of 12 inches every year.** *nope*
    - **Men can read smaller print than womenwomen can hear better than men.** *yup*

You'll Need—

- ☼ A sign on one wall of your room that says YUP.
- ☼ A sign on one wall of your room that says NOPE.

- **All your blood circulates through your body in the course of five minutes.** *nope*
- **People with high levels of intelligence have more zinc and copper in their hair than people with lower intelligence.** *yup*
- **Proportional to their weight, men are stronger than horses.** *yup*
- **Your nose and ears stop growing when you're in your teens.** *nope, they never stop growing*
- **Women get the hiccups more often than men.** *nope*
- **If you yelled for eight years, seven months, and six days, you would have produced enough sound energy to heat one cup of coffee.** *yup*
- **The human heart creates enough pressure while pumping to squirt blood 20 feet.** *nope, it's 30 feet!*
- **Banging your head against a wall uses 150 calories an hour.** *yup*
- **The strongest muscle in the body is the stomach.** *nope, it's the tongue*
- **It's impossible to sneeze with your eyes open.** *yup*
- **You can kill yourself by holding your breath.** *nope*
- **Every time you lick a stamp, you're consuming ⅒th of a calorie.** *yup*
- **Right-handed people live, on average, two years longer than left-handed people do.** *nope, they live nine years longer!*

- **The hyoid bone, in your throat, is the only bone in the body not attached to another bone.** *yup*
- **The average person falls asleep in 12 minutes.** *nope, seven minutes*

Choose a car salesman

If you're able to recruit two actors before your meeting (their gender doesn't matter) who will do a fantastic job, then have them perform both of the **Choose a Car Salesman** dramas (pages 90-91). Otherwise, feel free to recruit four volunteers (kids or adult leaders) right at the point you'll use these dramas, and just have them read their parts off the copies you give them. Try to pick kids who you know are good readers. It can be humiliating to young teens to read in front of a group if they're uncomfortable with reading. You also want to encourage the actors to ham it up.

All that thespian stuff aside, ask your group to watch these two dramas without much intro. Then perform the two bits in order (duh, Drama 1, then Drama 2!). Afterward thank your Oscar-deserving performers and ask—

You'll Need—

- ☻ Two or four actors (one pair per drama or a pair willing to do both dramas)
- ☻ Copies of the **Choose a Car Salesman** dramas (pages 90-91)
- ☻ Bibles
- ☻ Half sheets of paper
- ☻ Pens or pencils

☻ **Which of those salespeople would you rather buy a car from?**
The obvious answer is the second one.

☻ **Why?**
Because the first one doesn't have the experience to know what he or she's talking about.

☻ **Can you think of a time when someone was telling you about something they obviously hadn't experienced?**
See if any of your kids have a story to share. Or better yet, share an example of a time you tried to stupidly convince someone of something you hadn't experienced.

Now say something like—

Today we're talking about the portrait God gives us of himself as a human. Does anyone have any idea what those dramas would have to do with this idea?
A sharp kid might catch this connection—God has experienced being a human, just like the second salesperson had experienced driving fun cars. That makes God worthy of our trust—he knows what life is like for us.

Ask your group to turn to Hebrews 4:15-16, and read it together.

You could continue this point in a couple ways. If you have enough time, and especially if you use small groups, pass out a half-sheet of blank paper and something to write with to groups of kids, and ask them to rewrite the verse in their own words—as a group (just one person can write for the group). After each group has written a paraphrase, have them all read their work for the whole group.

Or, if you prefer, ask the whole group another difficult question—

☻ **Who can take a shot at telling us what that verse means?**

For we do not have a high priest who is unable to sympathize with our weaknesses, but we have one who has been tempted in every way, just as we are—yet was without sin. Let us then approach the throne of grace with confidence, so that we may receive mercy and find grace to help us in our time of need.
Hebrews 4:15-16

Jesus is the middleman between us and God. But he's not one who doesn't have a clue what life is like for us. He's gone through everything we have—temptation, emotion, troubles, pain. That should give us confidence that he'll really be there for us when we need him.

Either way, continue with these questions—

ᾦ What difference does it make that Jesus knows what it's like to be human?

You've already answered this question. But it's the core truth of the lesson and will be applied to your students' lives in the next section; so it's essential they grasp this. Don't let them get away with rote, churchy answers—those overly simplistic responses that don't reflect any thought or real life (like, "Well, it makes me happy," or "It gives me confidence").

ᾦ Why did Jesus bother being a human? Since he knows everything, shouldn't he know what it's like to be human without actually doing it?

This is a tricky question (hee-hee!). In fact—you take a crack at the answer!

Figure it out yet?

C'mon, no cheating! Think of an answer before you read any further!

Okay, here's a human answer to the question. (You'll probably have to summarize this for your kids, because they aren't likely to come up with this on their own.)

Obviously, the main point of Jesus becoming human was to offer us a restored relationship with God. He could have known—and probably did know—what it was like to be human prior to becoming one. But we needed to know that Jesus knows what it's like to be human. It gives us confidence that Jesus knows and understands what we're going through! This is way cool!

Ask your students to vote on which of these three statements is the *most* true. Actually they're all true, but the last one contains the most profound thought of truth. Let your kids try to persuade the others to agree with their choice.

ᾦ Jesus had to become a human so he could know what it's like for us.

ᾦ In becoming a human, Jesus proved he could do anything.

ᾦ In becoming a human, Jesus proved he was willing to come to us, rather than making us come to him.

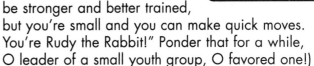

A dog's life

Have students divide into groups of about five. (Don't whine if your whole group *is* five kids. This isn't a competition. In fact, if you're concerned about being a small youth group, you need to rent the '80s movie *Meatballs*, starring Bill Murray, and listen to his speech near the end of the movie to the kid named Rudy he's coaching in long-distance running. He says something like, "The other runners might be stronger and better trained, but you're small and you can make quick moves. You're Rudy the Rabbit!" Ponder that for a while, O leader of a small youth group, O favored one!)

You'll Need—

ᾦ Blank paper
ᾦ Pens or pencils

Dogs, rabbits? Where was I? Oh yeah, ask your kids to think like a dog! Really. Tell them they should pretend that for one day they were able to become a dog—any kind of dog. As a group, they should come up with a list of things they learned from being Fido-for-a-day, and have one person write their ideas down on a blank piece of paper.

After a couple minutes, have each group report back to the whole group. Have the presenters speak in first person ("We learned that..."), and, if your group likes to get crazy, like a dog (Scooby-Doo talk).

Now you'll need to segue, something along these lines—

Obviously, you can't become a dog. And it's a bit silly to talk about becoming a human, since most of you already are one! But we should still be able to see how this characteristic of God's in us. I think the way it should show up in us is a willingness to go out of our way to connect with people, to show them love on their terms even when it's inconvenient for us.

Read this short list of mini-case studies, and ask your students to vote on which ones are putting this principle into practice (if you wanna get way fancy, you can tell them the $10 word for this—it's called being *incarnational*. They may have heard the term *God Incarnate*. You seminarians were way ahead of me on that one, weren't you?).

Jase taught himself how to build Web sites so he could hang out with Reuben, who was into Web sites, but didn't have many friends.
Oh, yeah, big time! Jase becomes a Web guy—for Reuben.

Brianne didn't want to go to the mall but went anyhow.
Brianne, honey, we don't know your motivation—how can we vote?

L'Tisha forced herself to listen to classical music until she could appreciate it, because she knew it was a big deal to her friend Lora.
You go, girl! Yes! L'Tisha becomes a classical music listener—for Lora.

Ty dreams of becoming a pro baseball player, so he practices with Greg, who's great at baseball, three days a week.
Nothing wrong with this, Ty, but you're not an example of this principle—sorry!

Sharina gives money to a homeless project in her city.
Sharina, you rock, but that doesn't mean you're an example of this principle.

TJ is the best ball player in gym class. But he gave up his job as the team captain today and had another guy pick the teams, a kid who never gets to do it.
Go TJ, you're an incarnational hero! TJ becomes a regular guy on the team—for the kid in his class.

Penny's mom is always stressed about keeping the house clean–especially because she works long hours and doesn't have time to clean it. Penny starts doing more around the house, even though she hates it.
Penny gets a sticker for her forehead! Penny becomes a housecleaner—for her mother.

Tommy pretended to be a dog.
Whatever!

Print it!

I'll become–

Pass out copies of **I'll Become Something!** (page 92), and pens or pencils for every little precious squirrel in the room. Ask them to fill in the blanks on this sheet, which forces them to both review the God-picture, and apply it to their lives. After a few minutes, have some willing kids read their statements to the whole group.

End in prayer, thanking God for becoming human for us, for giving us confidence in how we approach him! And ask for courage to carry out your *becoming* acts.

You'll Need—

- Copies of **I'll Become Something!** (page 92), cut in half
- Pens or pencils

Room decoration option
If you're using the decoration option described at the end of Lesson 1, add a large graphic of a person to your wall, maybe one that looks like the Mona Lisa. She looks like a human!

Choose a Car Salesman

drama 1

CAST
a car salesperson
a prospective buyer

(Buyer walks into store, salesperson stands to greet)

Salesperson: Hi, welcome to Joe Bob's Sweet Rides—where our motto is, "We've got the car of your dreams, and you'll leave in it, or my name isn't Joe Bob."

Buyer: Uh, is your name Joe Bob?

Salesperson: Well, no.

Buyer: So I probably won't leave with the car of my dreams?

Salesperson: Hey, it's just a motto—give me a break, huh?

Buyer: Whatever.

Salesperson: *(acting excited)* So, let's get to it! What kind of dream car do you have in mind today?

Buyer: Well, I'm really looking for a car that's fun to drive. Know what I mean?

Salesperson: Sure! I mean, kinda. Um, I think I know what you mean.

Buyer: Either you know what I mean or you don't.

Salesperson: Well, I've heard lots of people *talk* about cars that are fun to drive.

Buyer: But you've never driven a car that was fun?

Salesperson: Actually, I've never, well, I've never driven a car at all.

Buyer: What?!

Salesperson: So I've never driven a car. They kind of freak me out. What's the big deal?

Buyer: It's a bit hard to believe that you'd have any real input for me if you've never driven a car!

Salesperson: Well then, just pretend I've driven a car!

Buyer: I think I'll go somewhere else instead, Joe Bob.

Salesperson: My name isn't Joe Bob!

Choose a Car Salesman

drama 2

CAST
a car salesperson
a prospective buyer

(Buyer walks into store, salesperson stands to greet)

Salesperson: Hi, welcome to Pete's Chariots—where our motto is "We only sell what we'd drive!"

Buyer: Oh, well, what if I wouldn't drive what you'd want to drive?

Salesperson: It's just a slogan, of course, but we really do believe in our cars! What are you looking for?

Buyer: I'm tired of all the boring cars I've had. I want something that's really fun to drive!

Salesperson: I think I know what you mean—but tell me what a fun car is to you.

Buyer: It's gotta be fast—and take corners well. And it's gotta look really cool. You know, like a racecar.

Salesperson: I know exactly what you mean! I've driven lots of cars just like that!

Buyer: Oh yeah?

Salesperson: Well, I used to be a racecar driver. I've raced in Daytona, and I've raced Indy cars too.

Buyer: No way!

Salesperson: Way! My experience really helps me now when people say they want a fast, cool car. I know exactly what they mean!

Buyer: I guess so! Let me see your cars!

WiLDPAGE

i'll Become Something!

Fill in the blanks.

Jesus became a _____ for me, so I could _____.

I'll become a _____ for _____, by doing this: _____
_____
_____. I'll begin by_____
_____
_____. And I'll pray that the

result is

_____.

Signed _____ Date _____

- -

WiLDPAGE

i'll Become Something!

Fill in the blanks.

Jesus became a _____ for me, so I could _____.

I'll become a _____ for _____, by doing this: _____
_____
_____. I'll begin by_____
_____
_____. And I'll pray that the result

is _____.

Signed _____ Date _____

Resources from Youth Specialties

Youth Ministry Programming
Camps, Retreats, Missions, & Service Ideas (Ideas Library)
Compassionate Kids: Practical Ways to Involve Your Students in Mission and Service
Creative Bible Lessons from the Old Testament
Creative Bible Lessons in 1 & 2 Corinthians
Creative Bible Lessons in John: Encounters with Jesus
Creative Bible Lessons in Romans: Faith on Fire!
Creative Bible Lessons on the Life of Christ
Creative Bible Lessons in Psalms
Creative Junior High Programs from A to Z, Vol. 1 (A-M)
Creative Junior High Programs from A to Z, Vol. 2 (N-Z)
Creative Meetings, Bible Lessons, & Worship Ideas (Ideas Library)
Crowd Breakers & Mixers (Ideas Library)
Downloading the Bible Leader's Guide
Drama, Skits, & Sketches (Ideas Library)
Drama, Skits, & Sketches 2 (Ideas Library)
Dramatic Pauses
Everyday Object Lessons
Games (Ideas Library)
Games 2 (Ideas Library)
Good Sex: A Whole-Person Approach to Teenage Sexuality and God
Great Fundraising Ideas for Youth Groups
More Great Fundraising Ideas for Youth Groups
Great Retreats for Youth Groups
Holiday Ideas (Ideas Library)
Hot Illustrations for Youth Talks
More Hot Illustrations for Youth Talks
Still More Hot Illustrations for Youth Talks
Ideas Library on CD-ROM
Incredible Questionnaires for Youth Ministry
Junior High Game Nights
More Junior High Game Nights
Kickstarters: 101 Ingenious Intros to Just about Any Bible Lesson
Live the Life! Student Evangelism Training Kit
Memory Makers
The Next Level Leader's Guide
Play It! Over 150 Great Games for Youth Groups
Roaring Lambs
So What Am I Gonna Do with My Life? Leader's Guide
Special Events (Ideas Library)
Spontaneous Melodramas
Spontaneous Melodramas 2
Student Leadership Training Manual
Student Underground: An Event Curriculum on the Persecuted Church
Super Sketches for Youth Ministry
Talking the Walk
Videos That Teach
What Would Jesus Do? Youth Leader's Kit
Wild Truth Bible Lessons
Wild Truth Bible Lessons 2
Wild Truth Bible Lessons—Pictures of God
Wild Truth Bible Lessons—Pictures of God 2
Worship Services for Youth Groups

Professional Resources
Administration, Publicity, & Fundraising (Ideas Library)
Dynamic Communicators Workshop for Youth Workers
Equipped to Serve: Volunteer Youth Worker Training Course
Help! I'm a Junior High Youth Worker!
Help! I'm a Small-Group Leader!
Help! I'm a Sunday School Teacher!
Help! I'm a Volunteer Youth Worker!
How to Expand Your Youth Ministry
How to Speak to Youth...and Keep Them Awake at the Same Time
Junior High Ministry (Updated & Expanded)
The Ministry of Nurture: A Youth Worker's Guide to Discipling Teenagers
Postmodern Youth Ministry
Purpose-Driven Youth Ministry
Purpose-Driven Youth Ministry Training Kit
So That's Why I Keep Doing This! 52 Devotional Stories for Youth Workers
Teaching tho Biblc Creatively
A Youth Ministry Crash Course
Youth Ministry Management Tools
The Youth Worker's Handbook to Family Ministry

Academic Resources
Four Views of Youth Ministry & the Church
Starting Right: Thinking Theologically about Youth Ministry

Discussion Starters
Discussion & Lesson Starters (Ideas Library)
Discussion & Lesson Starters 2 (Ideas Library)
EdgeTV
Get 'Em Talking
Keep 'Em Talking!
Good Sex: A Whole-Person Approach to Teenage Sexuality & God
High School TalkSheets
More High School TalkSheets
High School TalkSheets from Psalms and Proverbs
Junior High TalkSheets
More Junior High TalkSheets
Junior High TalkSheets from Psalms and Proverbs
Real Kids: Short Cuts
Real Kids: The Real Deal—on Friendship, Loneliness, Racism, & Suicide
Real Kids: The Real Deal—on Sexual Choices, Family Matters, & Loss
Real Kids: The Real Deal—on Stressing Out, Addictive Behavior, Great Comebacks, & Violence
Real Kids: Word on the Street
Unfinished Sentences: 450 Tantalizing Statement-Starters to Get Teenagers Talking & Thinking
What If...? 450 Thought-Provoking Questions to Get Teenagers Talking, Laughing, and Thinking
Would You Rather...? 465 Provocative Questions to Get Teenagers Talking
Have You Ever...? 450 Intriguing Questions Guaranteed to Get Teenagers Talking

Art Source Clip Art
Stark Raving Clip Art (print)
Youth Group Activities (print)
Clip Art Library Version 2.0 (CD-ROM)

Digital Resources
Clip Art Library Version 2.0 (CD-ROM)
Ideas Library on CD-ROM
Youth Ministry Management Tools (CD-ROM)

Videos & Video Curricula
Dynamic Communicators Workshop for Youth Workers
EdgeTV
Equipped to Serve: Volunteer Youth Worker Training Course
Good Sex: A Whole-Person Approach to Teenage Sexuality & God
The Heart of Youth Ministry: A Morning with Mike Yaconelli
Live the Life! Student Evangelism Training Kit
Purpose-Driven Youth Ministry Training Kit
Real Kids: Short Cuts
Real Kids: The Real Deal—on Friendship, Loneliness, Racism, & Suicide
Real Kids: The Real Deal—on Sexual Choices, Family Matters, & Loss
Real Kids: The Real Deal—on Stressing Out, Addictive Behavior, Great Comebacks, & Violence
Real Kids: Word on the Street
Student Underground: An Event Curriculum on the Persecuted Church
Understanding Your Teenager Video Curriculum
Youth Ministry Outside the Lines: The Dangerous Wonder of Working with Teenagers

Student Resources
Downloading the Bible: A Rough Guide to the New Testament
Downloading the Bible: A Rough Guide to the Old Testament
Grow For It Journal
Grow For It Journal through the Scriptures
So What Am I Gonna Do with My Life? Journaling Workbook for Students
Spiritual Challenge Journal: The Next Level
Teen Devotional Bible
What Almost Nobody Will Tell You about Sex
What Would Jesus Do? Spiritual Challenge Journal
Wild Truth Journal for Junior Highers
Wild Truth Journal—Pictures of God